Global Trends 2015:

A Dialogue About the Future

Director of Central Intelligence

COSIMO-ON-DEMAND
NEW YORK

Global Trends 2015: A Dialogue About the Future

2005 Cosimo, Inc.

Global Trends 2015: A Dialogue About the Future is in the public domain and no copyright is claimed therein.

Visit our website at: www.cosimobooks.com

Library of Congress Cataloging-in-Publication Data
A catalog record for this book is available from the Library of Congress.

Cover design by www.wiselephant.com

ISBN: 1-59605-174-4

Global Trends 2015:
A Dialogue About the Future
With Nongovernment Experts

NIC 2000-02
December 2000

NIC 2000-02

Global Trends 2015:
A Dialogue About the Future With Nongovernment Experts

This paper was approved for publication by the National Foreign Intelligence Board under the authority of the Director of Central Intelligence.

Prepared under the direction of the National Intelligence Council.

December 2000

13 December 2000

From the Director of Central Intelligence

I am pleased to introduce Global Trends 2015, which takes a look at the world over the next 15 years from the perspective of the national security policymaker. This is not a traditional intelligence assessment, depending on classified sources and methods. Rather, it reflects an Intelligence Community fully engaged with outside experts in a constructive dialogue about the future. I want to encourage this lively exchange.

From the beginning of this ambitious project in fall 1999, we intended to make GT-2015 an unclassified assessment to be shared with the public. Experts from academia, think-tanks and the corporate world have made major contributions, and their reactions, along with those of other specialists who will see our work for the first time, will strengthen our continuing analysis of the issues covered in GT-2015. Grappling with the future is necessarily a work in progress that, I believe, should constantly seek new insights while testing and revising old judgments.

I hope that GT-2015 will contribute to a growing strategic dialogue in the US Government that will help our country meet the challenges and opportunities ahead. I look forward to your comments.

George J. Tenet

From the Chairman of the National Intelligence Council:

The National Intelligence Council (NIC), a small center of strategic thinking in the US Intelligence Community, launched *Global Trends 2015* to stimulate US policymakers to think "beyond their inboxes." This work expands the effort of *Global Trends 2010*, published in 1997 under the leadership of my predecessor, Professor Richard Cooper of Harvard.

We identify global "drivers" and estimate their impact on the world over the next 15 years—demography and natural resources, technology, globalization and governance, likely conflicts and prospects for international cooperation, and the role of the United States. The judgments flow from our best efforts to produce a comprehensive picture of the world in 2015. Analysis will help senior leaders better cope with, for example, the uncertainties involved with the decline of Russia, the emergence of China, or the political, economic and societal dynamics in the Middle East.

Global Trends 2015 should be seen as a work-in-progress, a flexible framework for thinking about the future that we will update and revise as conditions evolve. As such, we are pleased to share it with the public, confident that the feedback we receive will improve our understanding of the issues we treat. We welcome comments on all aspects of this study.

Global Trends 2015 is not a traditional intelligence product based on classic intelligence sources, methods and procedures. The National Intelligence Council gave overall direction to the year-long effort, assisted by colleagues from other intelligence agencies and offices. We sought out and drew heavily on experts outside the Intelligence Community to help us both identify the key drivers and assess their impact worldwide. Ultimately, however, the conclusions are our responsibility.

The NIC's Vice Chairman, Ellen Laipson, and I want to acknowledge the special contributions of several individuals. Enid Schoettle, my special adviser on the NIC, was a principal drafter and coordinator, and she was ably assisted by retired diplomat Richard Smith. The DCI Environmental and Societal Issues Center, led by Paul Frandano, made extensive, invaluable contributions. John Phillips, Chief Scientist of CIA, Directorate of Science and Technology, offered helpful suggestions. Tom Fingar of the State Department's Bureau of Intelligence and Research made important inputs, as did Ken Knight and Pat Neary of the Defense Intelligence Agency. All the regional and functional National Intelligence Officers (NIOs)—identified at the back page of this publication—contributed sections and provided insights in their areas of expertise. In the final stages of preparing the full text, Enid Schoettle and NIOs Stuart A. Cohen (with his crack staff), David F. Gordon, and Barry F. Lowenkron performed the critical service of integrating substantive comments and judgments.

We are particularly grateful to the Director of Central Intelligence, George Tenet, who encouraged us to take on this ambitious project and provided us with the necessary assistance to bring it to fruition.

John Gannon
Chairman

DI Design Center 377189AI 12-00

(U) **Note on Process**

In undertaking this comprehensive analysis, the NIC worked actively with a range of nongovernmental institutions and experts. We began the analysis with two workshops focusing on drivers and alternative futures, as the appendix describes. Subsequently, numerous specialists from academia and the private sector contributed to every aspect of the study, from demographics to developments in science and technology, from the global arms market to implications for the United States. Many of the judgments in this paper derive from our efforts to distill the diverse views expressed at these conferences or related workshops. Major conferences cosponsored by the NIC with other government and private centers in support of *Global Trends 2015* included:

- **Foreign Reactions to the Revolution in Military Affairs** (Georgetown University).

- **Evolution of the Nation-State** (University of Maryland).

- **Trends in Democratization** (CIA and academic experts).

- **American Economic Power** (Industry & Trade Strategies, San Francisco, CA).

- **Transformation of Defense Industries** (International Institute for Strategic Studies, London, UK).

- **Alternative Futures in War and Conflict** (Defense Intelligence Agency and Naval War College, Newport, RI, and CIA).

- **Out of the Box and Into the Future: A Dialogue Between Warfighters and Scientists on Far Future Warfare** (Potomac Institute, Arlington, VA).

- **Future Threat Technologies Symposium** (MITRE Corporation, McLean, VA).

- **The Global Course of the Information Revolution: Technological Trends** (RAND Corporation, Santa Monica, CA).

- **The Global Course of the Information Revolution: Political, Economic, and Social Consequences** (RAND Corporation, Santa Monica, CA).

- **The Middle East: The Media, Information Technology, and the Internet** (The National Defense University, Fort McNair, Washington, DC).

- **Global Migration Trends and Their Implications for the United States** (Carnegie Endowment for International Peace, Washington, DC).

- **Alternative Global Futures: 2000-2015** (Department of State/Bureau of Intelligence and Research and CIA's Global Futures Project).

In October 2000, the draft report was discussed with outside experts, including Richard Cooper and Joseph Nye (Harvard University), Richard Haass (Brookings Institution), James Steinberg (Markle Foundation), and Jessica Mathews (Carnegie Endowment for International Peace). Their comments and suggestions are incorporated in the report. Daniel Yergin (Cambridge Energy Research Associates) reviewed and commented on the final draft.

(U) Contents

Appendix

(U) Overview

Global Trends 2015:
A Dialogue About the Future
With Nongovernment Experts

Over the past 15 months, the National Intelligence Council (NIC), in close collaboration with US Government specialists and a wide range of experts outside the government, has worked to identify major drivers and trends that will shape the world of 2015.

The key drivers identified are:

(1) Demographics.

(2) Natural resources and environment.

(3) Science and technology.

(4) The global economy and globalization.

(5) National and international governance.

(6) Future conflict.

(7) The role of the United States.

In examining these drivers, several points should be kept in mind:

• No single driver or trend will dominate the global future in 2015.

• Each driver will have varying impacts in different regions and countries.

• The drivers are not necessarily mutually reinforcing; in some cases, they will work at cross-purposes.

Taken together, these drivers and trends intersect to create an integrated picture of the world of 2015, about which we can make projections with varying degrees of confidence and identify some troubling uncertainties of strategic importance to the United States.

The Methodology   *Global Trends 2015* provides a flexible framework to discuss and debate the future. The methodology is useful for our purposes, although admittedly inexact for the social scientist. Our purpose is to rise above short-term, tactical considerations and provide a longer-term, strategic perspective.

Judgments about demographic and natural resource trends are based primarily on informed extrapolation of existing trends. In contrast, many judgments about science and technology, economic growth, globalization, governance, and the nature of conflict represent a distillation of views of experts inside and outside the United States Government. The former are projections about natural phenomena, about which we can have fairly high confidence; the latter are more speculative because they are contingent upon the decisions that societies and governments will make.

The drivers we emphasize will have staying power. Some of the trends will persist; others will be less enduring and may change course over the time frame we consider. The major contribution of the National Intelligence Council (NIC), assisted by experts from the Intelligence Community, has been to harness US Government and nongovernmental specialists to identify drivers, to determine which ones matter most, to highlight key uncertainties, and to integrate analysis of these trends into a national security context. The result identifies issues for more rigorous analysis and quantification.

Revisiting Global Trends 2010: How Our Assessments Have Changed

Over the past four years, we have tested the judgments made in the predecessor, Global Trends 2010, *published in 1997.* Global Trends 2010 *was the centerpiece of numerous briefings, conferences, and public addresses. Various audiences were energetic in challenging, modifying or confirming our judgments. The lively debate that ensued has expanded our treatment of drivers, altered some projections we made in 1997, and matured our thinking overall—which was the essential purpose of this exercise.*

Global Trends 2015 *amplifies several drivers identified previously, and links them more closely to the trends we now project over the next 15 years. Some of the key changes include:*

- *Globalization has emerged as a more powerful driver.* GT 2015 *sees international economic dynamics—including developments in the* World Trade Organization—*and the spread of information technology as having much greater influence than portrayed in* GT 2010.

(continued)

- GT 2015 *assigns more significance to the importance of governance, notably the ability of states to deal with nonstate actors, both good and bad. GT 2015 pays attention both to the opportunities for cooperation between governments and private organizations and to the growing reach of international criminal and terrorist networks.*

- GT 2015 *includes a more careful examination of the likely role of science and technology as a driver of global developments. In addition to the growing significance of information technology, biotechnology and other technologies carry much more weight in the present assessment.*

- *The effect of the United States as the preponderant power is introduced in* GT 2015. *The US role as a global driver has emerged more clearly over the past four years, particularly as many countries debate the impact of "US hegemony" on their domestic and foreign policies.*

- GT 2015 *provides a more complete discussion of natural resources including food, water, energy, and the environment. It discusses, for example, the over three billion individuals who will be living in water-stressed regions from North China to Africa and the implications for conflict. The linkage between energy availability, price, and distribution is more thoroughly explored.*

- GT 2015 *emphasizes interactions among the drivers. For example, we discuss the relationship between S&T, military developments, and the potential for conflict.*

- *In the regional sections,* GT 2015 *makes projections about the impact of the spread of information, the growing power of China, and the declining power of Russia.*

Events and trends in key states and regions over the last four years have led us to revise some projections substantially in GT 2015.

- GT 2010 *did not foresee the global financial crisis of 1997-98;* GT 2015 *takes account of obstacles to economic development in East Asia, though the overall projections remain fairly optimistic.*

(continued)

The Drivers and Trends

Demographics

World population in 2015 will be 7.2 billion, up from 6.1 billion in the year 2000, and in most countries, people will live longer. Ninety-five percent of the increase will be in developing countries, nearly all in rapidly expanding urban areas. Where political systems are brittle, the combination of population growth and urbanization will foster instability. Increasing lifespans will have significantly divergent impacts.

• In the advanced economies—and a growing number of emerging market countries—declining birthrates and aging will combine to increase health care and pension costs while reducing the relative size of the working population, straining the social contract, and leaving significant shortfalls in the size and capacity of the work force.

• In some developing countries, these same trends will combine to expand the size of the working population and reduce the youth bulge—increasing the potential for economic growth and political stability.

Natural Resources and Environment	Overall food production will be adequate to feed the world's growing population, but poor infrastructure and distribution, political instability, and chronic poverty will lead to malnourishment in parts of Sub-Saharan Africa. The potential for famine will persist in countries with repressive government policies or internal conflicts. Despite a 50 percent increase in global energy demand, energy resources will be sufficient to meet demand; the latest estimates suggest that 80 percent of the world's available oil and 95 percent of its gas remain underground.

- Although the Persian Gulf region will remain the world's largest single source of oil, the global energy market is likely to encompass two relatively distinct patterns of regional distribution: one serving consumers (including the United States) from Atlantic Basin reserves; and the other meeting the needs of primarily Asian customers (increasingly China and India) from Persian Gulf supplies and, to a lesser extent, the Caspian region and Central Asia.

- In contrast to food and energy, water scarcities and allocation will pose significant challenges to governments in the Middle East, Sub-Saharan Africa, South Asia, and northern China. Regional tensions over water will be heightened by 2015.

Science and Technology	Fifteen years ago, few predicted the profound impact of the revolution in information technology. Looking ahead another 15 years, the world will encounter more quantum leaps in information technology (IT) and in other areas of science and technology. The continuing diffusion of information technology and new applications of biotechnology will be at the crest of the wave. IT will be the major building block for international commerce and for empowering nonstate actors. Most experts agree that the IT revolution represents the most significant global transformation since the Industrial Revolution beginning in the mid-eighteenth century.

- The integration—or fusion—of continuing revolutions in information technology, biotechnology, materials science, and nanotechnology will generate a dramatic increase in investment in technology, which will further stimulate innovation within the more advanced countries.

- Older technologies will continue lateral "sidewise development" into new markets and applications through 2015, benefiting US allies and adversaries around the world who are interested in acquiring early generation ballistic missile and weapons of mass destruction (WMD) technologies.

- Biotechnology will drive medical breakthroughs that will enable the world's wealthiest people to improve their health and increase their longevity dramatically. At the same time, genetically modified crops will offer the potential to improve nutrition among the world's one billion malnourished people.

- Breakthroughs in materials technology will generate widely available products that are multi-functional, environmentally safe, longer lasting, and easily adapted to particular consumer requirements.

- Disaffected states, terrorists, proliferators, narcotraffickers, and organized criminals will take advantage of the new high-speed information environment and other advances in technology to integrate their illegal activities and compound their threat to stability and security around the world.

The Global Economy and Globalization

The networked global economy will be driven by rapid and largely unrestricted flows of information, ideas, cultural values, capital, goods and services, and people: that is, globalization. This globalized economy will be a net contributor to increased political stability in the world in 2015, although its reach and benefits will not be universal. In contrast to the Industrial Revolution, the process of globalization is more compressed. Its evolution will be rocky, marked by chronic financial volatility and a widening economic divide.

- The global economy, overall, will return to the high levels of growth reached in the 1960s and early 1970s. Economic growth will be driven by political pressures for higher living standards, improved economic policies, rising foreign trade and investment, the diffusion of information technologies, and an increasingly dynamic private sector. Potential brakes on the global economy—such as a sustained financial crisis or prolonged disruption of energy supplies—could undo this optimistic projection.

- Regions, countries, and groups feeling left behind will face deepening economic stagnation, political instability, and cultural alienation. They will foster political, ethnic, ideological, and religious extremism, along with the violence that often accompanies it. They will force the United States and other developed countries to remain focused on "old-world" challenges while concentrating on the implications of "new-world" technologies at the same time.

National and International Governance

States will continue to be the dominant players on the world stage, but governments will have less and less control over flows of information, technology, diseases, migrants, arms, and financial transactions, whether licit or illicit, across their borders. Nonstate actors ranging from business firms to nonprofit organizations will play increasingly larger roles in both national and international affairs. The quality of governance, both nationally and internationally, will substantially determine how well states and societies cope with these global forces.

- States with competent governance, including the United States, will adapt government structures to a dramatically changed global environment— making them better able to engage with a more interconnected world. The responsibilities of once "semiautonomous" government agencies increasingly will intersect because of the transnational nature of national security priorities and because of the clear requirement for interdisciplinary policy responses. Shaping the complex, fast-moving world of 2015 will require reshaping traditional government structures.

- Effective governance will increasingly be determined by the ability and agility to form partnerships to exploit increased information flows, new technologies, migration, and the influence of nonstate actors. Most but not all countries that succeed will be representative democracies.

- States with ineffective and incompetent governance not only will fail to benefit from globalization, but in some instances will spawn conflicts at home and abroad, ensuring an even wider gap between regional winners and losers than exists today.

Globalization will increase the transparency of government decision-making, complicating the ability of authoritarian regimes to maintain control, but also complicating the traditional deliberative processes of democracies. Increasing migration will create influential diasporas, affecting policies, politics and even national identity in many countries. Globalization also will create increasing demands for international cooperation on transnational issues, but the response of both states and international organizations will fall short in 2015.

Future Conflict   The United States will maintain a strong technological edge in IT-driven "battlefield awareness" and in precision-guided weaponry in 2015. The United States will face three types of threats:

- Asymmetric threats in which state and nonstate adversaries avoid direct engagements with the US military but devise strategies, tactics, and weapons—some improved by "sidewise" technology—to minimize US strengths and exploit perceived weaknesses;

- Strategic WMD threats, including nuclear missile threats, in which (barring significant political or economic changes) Russia, China, most likely North Korea, probably Iran, and possibly Iraq have the capability to strike the United States, and the potential for unconventional delivery of WMD by both states or nonstate actors also will grow; and

- Regional military threats in which a few countries maintain large military forces with a mix of Cold War and post-Cold War concepts and technologies.

The risk of war among developed countries will be low. The international community will continue, however, to face conflicts around the world, ranging from relatively frequent small-scale internal upheavals to less frequent regional interstate wars. The potential for conflict will arise from rivalries in Asia, ranging from India-Pakistan to China-Taiwan, as well as among the antagonists in the Middle East. Their potential lethality will grow, driven by the availability of WMD, longer-range missile delivery systems and other technologies.

Internal conflicts stemming from religious, ethnic, economic or political disputes will remain at current levels or even increase in number. The United Nations and regional organizations will be called upon to manage such conflicts because major states—stressed by domestic concerns, perceived risk of failure, lack of political will, or tight resources—will minimize their direct involvement.

Export control regimes and sanctions will be less effective because of the diffusion of technology, porous borders, defense industry consolidations, and reliance upon foreign markets to maintain profitability. Arms and weapons technology transfers will be more difficult to control.

- Prospects will grow that more sophisticated weaponry, including weapons of mass destruction—indigenously produced or externally acquired—will get into the hands of state and nonstate belligerents, some hostile to the United States. The likelihood will increase over this period that WMD will be used either against the United States or its forces, facilities, and interests overseas.

Role of the United States

The United States will continue to be a major force in the world community. US global economic, technological, military, and diplomatic influence will be unparalleled among nations as well as regional and international organizations in 2015. This power not only will ensure America's preeminence, but also will cast the United States as a key driver of the international system.

The United States will continue to be identified throughout the world as the leading proponent and beneficiary of globalization. US economic actions, even when pursued for such domestic goals as adjusting interest rates, will have a major global impact because of the tighter integration of global markets by 2015.

- The United States will remain in the vanguard of the technological revolution from information to biotechnology and beyond.

- Both allies and adversaries will factor continued US military pre-eminence in their calculations of national security interests and ambitions.

- Some states—adversaries and allies—will try at times to check what they see as American "hegemony." Although this posture will not translate into strategic, broad-based and enduring anti-US coalitions, it will lead to tactical alignments on specific policies and demands for a greater role in international political and economic institutions.

Diplomacy will be more complicated. Washington will have greater difficulty harnessing its power to achieve specific foreign policy goals: the US Government will exercise a smaller and less powerful part of the overall economic and cultural influence of the United States abroad.

- In the absence of a clear and overriding national security threat, the United States will have difficulty drawing on its economic prowess to advance its foreign policy agenda. The top priority of the American private sector, which will be central to maintaining the US economic and technological lead, will be financial profitability, not foreign policy objectives.

- The United States also will have greater difficulty building coalitions to support its policy goals, although the international community will often turn to Washington, even if reluctantly, to lead multilateral efforts in real and potential conflicts.

- There will be increasing numbers of important actors on the world stage to challenge and check—as well as to reinforce—US leadership: countries such as China, Russia, India, Mexico, and Brazil; regional organizations such as the European Union; and a vast array of increasingly powerful multinational corporations and nonprofit organizations with their own interests to defend in the world.

Key Uncertainties: Technology Will Alter Outcomes

Examining the interaction of these drivers and trends points to some major uncertainties that will only be clarified as events occur and leaders make policy decisions that cannot be foreseen today. We cite eight transnational and regional issues for which the future, according to our trends analysis, is too tough to call with any confidence or precision.

- **These are high-stakes, national security issues that will require continuous analysis and, in the view of our conferees, periodic policy review in the years ahead.**

Science and Technology

We know that the possibility is greater than ever that the revolution in science and technology will improve the quality of life. What we know about this revolution is exciting. Advances in science and technology will generate dramatic breakthroughs in agriculture and health and in leap-frog applications, such as universal wireless cellular communications, which already are networking developing countries that never had land-lines. What we do not know about the S&T revolution, however, is staggering. We do not know to what extent technology will benefit, or further disadvantage, disaffected national populations, alienated ethnic and religious groups, or the less developed countries. We do not know to what degree lateral or "sidewise" technology will increase the threat from low technology countries and groups. One certainty is that progression will not be linear. Another is that as future technologies emerge, people will lack full awareness of their wider economic, environmental, cultural, legal, and moral impact—or the continuing potential for research and development.

Advances in science and technology will pose national security challenges of uncertain character and scale.

- Increasing reliance on computer networks is making critical US infrastructures more attractive as targets. Computer network operations today offer new options for attacking the United States within its traditional continental sanctuary—potentially anonymously and with selective effects. Nevertheless, we do not know how quickly or effectively such adversaries as terrorists or disaffected states will develop the tradecraft to use cyber warfare tools and technology, or, in fact, whether cyber warfare will ever evolve into a decisive combat arm.

- Rapid advances and diffusion of biotechnology, nanotechnology, and the materials sciences, moreover, will add to the capabilities of our adversaries to engage in biological warfare or bio-terrorism.

Asymmetric Warfare

As noted earlier, most adversaries will recognize the information advantage and military superiority of the United States in 2015. Rather than acquiesce to any potential US military domination, they will try to circumvent or minimize US strengths and exploit perceived weaknesses. IT-driven globalization will significantly increase interaction among terrorists, narcotraffickers, weapons proliferators, and organized criminals, who in a networked world will have greater access to information, to technology, to finance, to sophisticated deception-and-denial techniques and to each other. Such asymmetric approaches—whether undertaken by states or nonstate actors—will become the dominant characteristic of most threats to the US homeland. They will be a defining challenge for US strategy, operations, and force development, and they will require that strategy to maintain focus on traditional, low-technology threats as well as the capacity of potential adversaries to harness elements of proliferating advanced technologies. At the same time, we do not know the extent to which adversaries, state and nonstate, might be influenced or deterred by other geopolitical, economic, technological, or diplomatic factors in 2015.

The Global Economy   Although the outlook for the global economy appears strong, achieving broad and sustained high levels of global growth will be contingent on avoiding several potential brakes to growth. These include:

The US economy suffers a sustained downturn. Given its large trade deficit and low domestic savings, the US economy—the most important driver of recent global growth—is vulnerable to a loss of international confidence in its growth prospects that could lead to a sharp downturn, which, if long lasting, would have deleterious economic and policy consequences for the rest of the world.

Europe and Japan fail to manage their demographic challenges. European and Japanese populations are aging rapidly, requiring more than 110 million new workers by 2015 to maintain current dependency ratios between the working population and retirees. Conflicts over social services or immigration policies in major European states could dampen economic growth.

China and/or India fail to sustain high growth. China's ambitious goals for reforming its economy will be difficult to achieve: restructuring state-owned enterprises, cleaning up and transforming the banking system, and cutting the government's employment rolls in half. Growth would slow if these reforms go off-track. Failure by India to implement reforms would prevent it from achieving sustained growth.

Emerging market countries fail to reform their financial institutions. Many emerging market countries have not yet undertaken the financial reforms needed to help them survive the next economic crisis. Absent such reform, a series of future economic crises in emerging market countries probably will dry up the capital flows crucial for high rates of economic growth.

Global energy supplies suffer a major disruption. Turbulence in global energy supplies would have a devastating effect. Such a result could be driven by conflict among key energy-producing states, sustained internal instability in two or more major energy-producing states, or major terrorist actions.

The Middle East   Global trends from demography and natural resources to globalization and governance appear generally negative for the Middle East. Most regimes are change-resistant. Many are buoyed by continuing energy revenues and will not be inclined to make the necessary reforms, including in basic education, to change this unfavorable picture.

- Linear trend analysis shows little positive change in the region, raising the prospects for increased demographic pressures, social unrest, religious and ideological extremism, and terrorism directed both at the regimes and at their Western supporters.

- Nonlinear developments—such as the sudden rise of a Web-connected opposition, a sharp and sustained economic downturn, or, conversely, the emergence of enlightened leaders committed to good governance—might change outcomes in individual countries. Political changes in Iran in the late 1990s are an example of such nonlinear development.

China   Estimates of developments in China over the next 15 years are fraught with unknowables. Working against China's aspirations to sustain economic growth while preserving its political system is an array of political, social, and economic pressures that will increasingly challenge the regime's legitimacy, and perhaps its survival.

- The sweeping structural changes required by China's entry into the World Trade Organization (WTO) and the broader demands of economic globalization and the information revolution will generate significantly new levels and types of social and economic disruption that will only add to an already wide range of domestic and international problems.

Nevertheless, China need not be overwhelmed by these problems. China has proven politically resilient, economically dynamic, and increasingly assertive in positioning itself for a leadership role in East Asia. Its long-term military program in particular suggests that Beijing wants to have the capability to achieve its territorial objectives, outmatch its neighbors, and constrain US power in the region.

- We do not rule out the introduction of enough political reform by 2015 to allow China to adapt to domestic pressure for change and to continue to grow economically.

Two conditions, in the view of many specialists, would lead to a major security challenge for the United States and its allies in the region: a weak, disintegrating China, or an assertive China willing to use its growing economic wealth and military capabilities to pursue its strategic advantage in the region. These opposite extremes bound a more commonly held view among experts that China will continue to see peace as essential to its economic growth and internal stability.

Russia

Between now and 2015, Moscow will be challenged even more than today to adjust its expectations for world leadership to its dramatically reduced resources. Whether the country can make the transition in adjusting ends to means remains an open and critical question, according to most experts, as does the question of the character and quality of Russian governance and economic policies. The most likely outcome is a Russia that remains internally weak and institutionally linked to the international system primarily through its permanent seat on the UN Security Council. In this view, whether Russia can adjust to this diminished status in a manner that preserves rather than upsets regional stability is also uncertain. The stakes for both Europe and the United States will be high, although neither will have the ability to determine the outcome for Russia in 2015. Russian governance will be the critical factor.

Japan

The first uncertainty about Japan is whether it will carry out the structural reforms needed to resume robust economic growth and to slow its decline relative to the rest of East Asia, particularly China. The second uncertainty is whether Japan will alter its security policy to allow Tokyo to maintain a stronger military and more reciprocal relationship with the United States. Experts agree that Japanese governance will be the key driver in determining the outcomes.

India

Global trends conflict significantly in India. The size of its population—1.2 billion by 2015—and its technologically driven economic growth virtually dictate that India will be a rising regional power. The unevenness of its internal economic growth, with a growing gap between rich and poor, and serious questions about the fractious nature of its politics, all cast doubt on how powerful India will be by 2015. Whatever its degree of power, India's rising ambition will further strain its relations with China, as well as complicate its ties with Russia, Japan, and the West—and continue its nuclear standoff with Pakistan.

Key Challenges to Governance: People Will Decide

Global Trends 2015 identifies governance as a major driver for the future and assumes that all trends we cite will be influenced, for good or bad, by decisions of people. The inclusion of the United States as a driver—both the US Government as well as US for-profit and nonprofit organizations—is based on the general assumption that the actions of nonstate actors as well as governments will shape global outcomes in the years ahead.

An integrated trend analysis suggests at least four related conclusions:

National Priorities Will Matter

• To prosper in the global economy of 2015, governments will have to invest more in technology, in public education, and in broader participation in government to include increasingly influential nonstate actors. The extent to which governments around the world are doing these things today gives some indication of where they will be in 2015.

US Responsibilities Will Cover the World, Old and New

• The United States and other developed countries will be challenged in 2015 to lead the fast-paced technological revolution while, at the same time, maintaining military, diplomatic, and intelligence capabilities to deal with traditional problems and threats from low-technology countries and groups. The United States, as a global power, will have little choice but to engage leading actors and confront problems on both sides of the widening economic and digital divides in the world of 2015, when globalization's benefits will be far from global.

US Foreign Priorities Will be More Transnational

• International or multilateral arrangements increasingly will be called upon in 2015 to deal with growing transnational problems from economic and financial volatility; to legal and illegal migration; to competition for scarce natural resources such as water; to humanitarian, refugee, and environmental crises; to terrorism, narcotrafficking, and weapons proliferation; and to both regional conflicts and cyber threats. And when international cooperation—or international governance—comes up short, the United States and other developed countries will have to broker solutions among a wide array of international players—including governments at all levels, multinational corporations, and nonprofit organizations.

National Governments Will be More Transparent

• To deal with a transnational agenda and an interconnected world in 2015, governments will have to develop greater communication and collaboration between national security and domestic policy agencies. Interagency cooperation will be essential to understanding transnational threats and to developing interdisciplinary strategies to counter them. Consequence management of a biological warfare (BW) attack, for example, would require close coordination among a host of US Government agencies, foreign governments, US state and municipal governments, the military, the medical community, and the media.

Discussion

Global Trends 2015:
A Dialogue About the Future
With Nongovernment Experts

The international system in 2015 will be shaped by seven global drivers and related trends: population; natural resources and the environment; science and technology; the global economy and globalization; national and international governance; the nature of conflict; and the role of the United States. These trends will influence the capacities, priorities, and behavior of states and societies and thus substantially define the international security environment.

Population Trends

The world in 2015 will be populated by some 7.2 billion people, up from 6.1 billion in the year 2000. The rate of world population growth, however, will have diminished from 1.7 percent annually in 1985, to 1.3 percent today, to approximately 1 percent in 2015.

Increased life expectancy and falling fertility rates will contribute to a shift toward an aging population in high-income developed countries. Beyond that, demographic trends will sharply diverge. More than 95 percent of the increase in world population will be found in developing countries, nearly all in rapidly expanding urban areas.

- India's population will grow from 900 million to more than 1.2 billion by 2015; Pakistan's probably will swell from 140 million now to about 195 million.

- Some countries in Africa with high rates of AIDS will experience reduced population growth or even declining populations despite relatively high birthrates. In South Africa, for example, the population is projected to drop from 43.4 million in 2000 to 38.7 million in 2015.

Russia and many post-Communist countries of Eastern Europe will have declining populations. As a result of high mortality and low birthrates, Russia's population may drop from its current 146 million to as low as 130 to 135 million in 2015, while the neighboring states of Central Asia will experience continued population growth. In Japan and West European countries such as Italy and Spain, populations also will decline in the absence of dramatic increases in birthrates or immigration.

- North America, Australia, and New Zealand—the traditional magnets for migrants—will continue to have the highest rates of population growth among the developed countries, with annual population growth rates between 0.7 percent and 1.0 percent.

Divergent Aging Patterns
In developed countries and many of the more advanced developing countries, the declining ratio of working people to retirees will strain social services, pensions, and health systems. Governments will seek to mitigate the problem through such measures as delaying retirement, encouraging greater participation in the work

Global Population: 1950-2015

Total

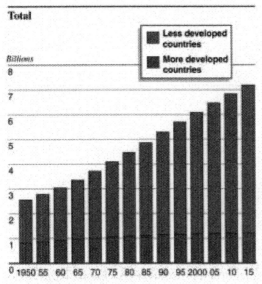

Source: US Bureau of the Census.

Growth Rates

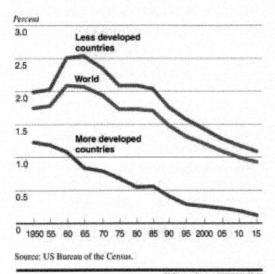

Source: US Bureau of the Census.

DI Design Center 375777A 09-00

force by women, and relying on migrant workers. Dealing effectively with declining dependency ratios is likely to require more extensive measures than most governments will be prepared to undertake. The shift towards a greater proportion of older voters will change the political dynamics in these countries in ways difficult to foresee.

At the same time, "youth bulges" will persist in some developing countries, notably in Sub-Saharan Africa and a few countries in Latin America and the Middle East. A high proportion of young people will be destabilizing, particularly when combined with high unemployment or communal tension.

Movement of People

Two major trends in the movement of people will characterize the next 15 years—urbanization and cross-border migration—each of which poses both opportunities and challenges.

The ratio of urban to rural dwellers is steadily increasing. By 2015 more than half of the world's population will be urban. The number of people living in mega-cities—those containing more than 10 million inhabitants—will double to more than 400 million.

- Urbanization will provide many countries the opportunity to tap the information revolution and other technological advances.

- The explosive growth of cities in developing countries will test the capacity of governments to stimulate the investment required to generate jobs and to provide the services, infrastructure, and social supports necessary to sustain livable and stable environments.

Divergent demographic trends, the globalization of labor markets, and political instability and conflict will fuel a dramatic increase in the

Growth in Megacities[a]

[a]Cities containing more than
10 million inhabitants.

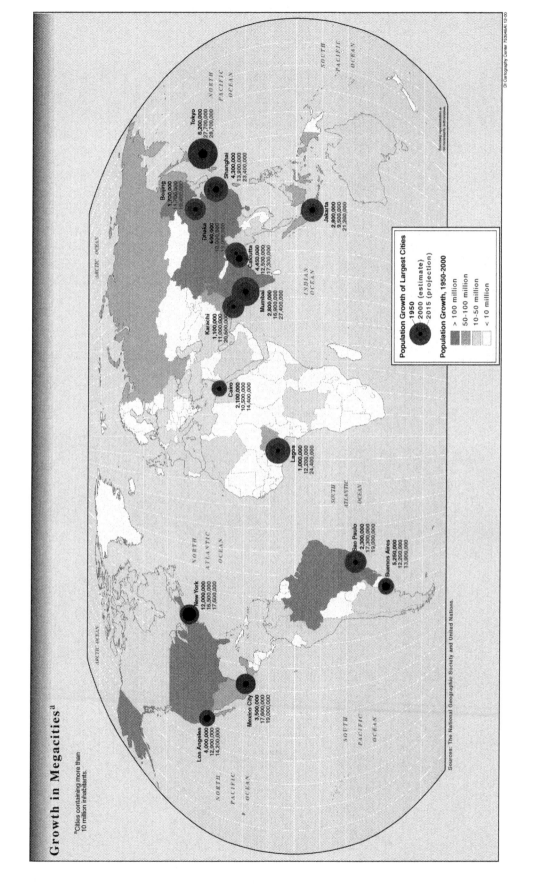

Population Growth of Largest Cities

- 1950
- 2000 (estimate)
- 2015 (projection)

Population Growth, 1950-2000

- \> 100 million
- 50-100 million
- 10-50 million
- \< 10 million

Tokyo
6,200,000
27,700,000
28,700,000

Shanghai
4,300,000
13,900,000
23,400,000

Beijing
1,700,000
11,700,000
19,400,000

Dhaka
400,000
10,900,000
19,000,000

Calcutta
4,450,000
12,900,000
17,300,000

Jakarta
2,900,000
9,500,000
21,200,000

Mumbai
2,900,000
16,900,000
27,400,000

Karachi
1,100,000
11,000,000
20,600,000

Cairo
2,100,000
10,500,000
14,400,000

Lagos
1,000,000
12,200,000
24,400,000

Sao Paulo
2,300,000
17,300,000
19,000,000

Buenos Aires
5,250,000
12,200,000
13,900,000

New York
12,000,000
16,500,000
17,600,000

Mexico City
3,500,000
17,600,000
19,000,000

Los Angeles
4,000,000
12,900,000
14,300,000

Sources: The National Geographic Society and United Nations.

Regional Population: 1950-2015

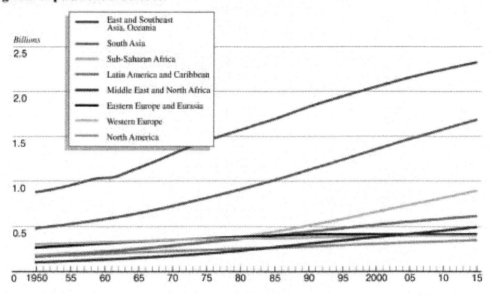

Billions

Legend:
- East and Southeast Asia, Oceania
- South Asia
- Sub-Saharan Africa
- Latin America and Caribbean
- Middle East and North Africa
- Eastern Europe and Eurasia
- Western Europe
- North America

Source: US Bureau of the Census.

global movement of people through 2015. Legal and illegal migrants now account for more than 15 percent of the population in more than 50 countries. These numbers will grow substantially and will increase social and political tension and perhaps alter national identities even as they contribute to demographic and economic dynamism.

States will face increasing difficulty in managing migration pressures and flows, which will number several million people annually. Over the next 15 years, migrants will seek to move:

- To North America primarily from Latin America and East and South Asia.

- To Europe primarily from North Africa and the Middle East, South Asia, and the post-Communist states of Eastern Europe and Eurasia.

- From the least to the most developed countries of Asia, Latin America, the Middle East, and Sub-Saharan Africa.

For high-income receiving countries, migration will relieve labor shortages and otherwise ensure continuing economic vitality. EU countries and Japan will need large numbers of new workers because of aging populations and low birthrates. Immigration will complicate political and social integration: some political parties will continue to mobilize popular sentiment against migrants, protesting the strain on social services and the difficulties in assimilation. European countries and Japan will face difficult dilemmas in seeking to reconcile protection of national borders and cultural identity with the need to address growing demographic and labor market imbalances.

Regional Population by Age Group: 2000 and 2015

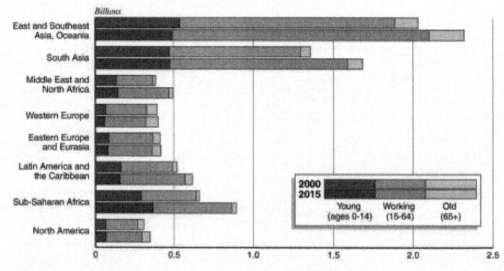

Billions

Source: US Bureau of the Census.

DI Design Center 375779/AI 09-00

For low-income receiving countries, mass migration resulting from civil conflict, natural disasters, or economic crises will strain local infrastructures, upset ethnic balances, and spark ethnic conflict. Illegal migration will become a more contentious issue between and among governments.

For low-income sending countries, mass migration will relieve pressures from unemployed and underemployed workers and generate significant remittances. Migrants will function as ethnic lobbies on behalf of sending-country interests, sometimes supporting armed conflicts in their home countries, as in the cases of the Albanian, Kurdish, Tamil, Armenian, Eritrean, and Ethiopian diasporas. At the same time, emigration increasingly will deprive low-income sending countries of their educated elites. An estimated 1.5 million skilled expatriates from developing countries already are employed in high-income countries. This brain drain from low-income to high-income countries is likely to intensify over the next 15 years.

Health

Disparities in health status between developed and developing countries—particularly the least developed countries—will persist and widen. In developed countries, major inroads against a variety of maladies will be achieved by 2015 as a result of generous health spending and major medical advances. The revolution in biotechnology holds the promise of even more dramatic improvements in health status. Noninfectious diseases will pose greater challenges to health in developed countries than will infectious diseases. Progress against infectious diseases, nevertheless, will encounter some setbacks as a result of growing microbial resistance to antibiotics and the accelerating

24

Countries With Youth Bulges in 2000 and 2015[a]

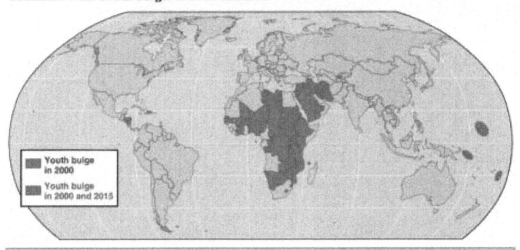

Latin America	Sub-Saharan Africa		Middle East	Asia/Pacific
Dominican Republic	Benin	Mali	Gaza Strip	Marshall Islands
Grenada	Botswana	Mozambique	Jordan	Solomon Islands
Haiti	Burkina Faso	Namibia	Lebanon	Tonga
Honduras	Burundi	Niger	Libya	
Nicaragua	Central African Republic	Nigeria	Iran	
	Chad	Rwanda	Iraq	
	Comoros	Sao Tome and	Saudi Arabia[b]	
	Congo, Democratic	Principe	Syria	
	Republic of the	Senegal	West Bank	
	Congo, Republic of	Sudan	Yemen	
	Cote d'Ivoire	Swaziland		
	Eritrea	Tanzania		
	Ethiopia	Togo		
	Kenya	Uganda		
	Lesotho[c]	Zambia		
	Malawi	Zimbabwe		

[a] A country is considered to have a youth bulge if the ratio of the population aged 15 to 29 to the population aged 30 to 54 exceeds 1.27.

[b] Saudi citizens only; does not include the large number of guest workers.

[c] Lesotho did not have a youth bulge in 2000.

DI Cartography Center 753973AI (R00053) 12-00

pace of international movement of people and products that facilitate the spread of infectious diseases.

Developing countries, by contrast, are likely to experience a surge in both infectious and non-infectious diseases and in general will have inadequate health care capacities and spending.

- Tuberculosis, malaria, hepatitis, and particularly AIDS will continue to increase rapidly. AIDS and TB together are likely to account for the majority of deaths in most developing countries.

AIDS will be a major problem not only in Africa but also in India, Southeast Asia, several countries formerly part of the Soviet Union, and possibly China.

- AIDS will reduce economic growth by up to 1 percent of GDP per year and consume more than 50 percent of health budgets in the hardest-hit countries.

- AIDS and such associated diseases as TB will have a destructive impact on families and society. In some African countries, average

A campaign in Abidjan, Cote d'Ivoire (Ivory Coast), to raise public awareness of AIDS ("SIDA" in French) has been effective in reducing levels in some countries. In Sub-Saharan Africa and parts of East and Southeast Asia, AIDS will have devastating effects during the next 15 years.

DI Design Center 376587A1 10-00

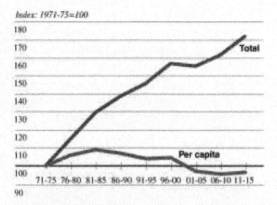

Global Grain Production: 1971-2015

Index: 1971-75=100

Sources: International Food Policy Research Institute, October 1999, US Bureau of the Census, and CIA.

DI Design Center 375781A1 06-00

lifespans will be reduced by as much as 30 to 40 years, generating more than 40 million orphans and contributing to poverty, crime, and instability.

- AIDS, other diseases, and health problems will hurt prospects for transition to democratic regimes as they undermine civil society, hamper the evolution of sound political and economic institutions, and intensify the struggle for power and resources.

Natural Resources and Environment

Food

Driven by advances in agricultural technologies, world food grain production and stocks in 2015 will be adequate to meet the needs of a growing world population. Despite the overall adequacy of food, problems of distribution and availability will remain.

- The number of chronically malnourished people in conflict-ridden Sub-Saharan Africa will increase by more than 20 percent over the next 15 years.

- The potential for famine will still exist where the combination of repressive government or internal conflict and persistent natural disasters prevents or limits relief efforts, as in Somalia in the early 1990s and North Korea more recently.

- Donors will become more reluctant to provide relief when the effort might become embroiled in military conflict.

The use of genetically modified crops has great potential for meeting the nutrition needs of the poor in developing countries. Popular and political opposition in the EU countries and, to a lesser extent, in the United States, however, has clouded the prospects for applying this technology.

26

Villagers in Bhaktapur, Nepal, use water from a well for drinking and bathing. Access to clean water will be a major health problem in many countries by 2015. Another will be the availability of adequate water supplies as water tables fall, agricultural demands rise with population growth, and the water requirements of rapidly expanding cities increase.

DI Design Center 375591AI 10-00

Traffic in Phnom Penh, Cambodia, outside the central market. By 2015 more than half the world's population will be urban. Most of the increase in urban populations will be in developing countries, challenging the capacities of governments to provide services, infrastructure, and the social support needed to sustain a livable environment.

DI Design Center 375589AI 10-00

Water

By 2015 nearly half the world's population— more than 3 billion people—will live in countries that are "water-stressed"—have less than 1,700 cubic meters of water per capita per year—mostly in Africa, the Middle East, South Asia, and northern China.

In the developing world, 80 percent of water usage goes into agriculture, a proportion that is not sustainable; and in 2015 a number of developing countries will be unable to maintain their levels of irrigated agriculture. Overpumping of groundwater in many of the world's important grain-growing regions will be an increasing problem; about 1,000 tons of water are needed to produce a ton of grain.

• The water table under some of the major grain-producing areas in northern China is falling at a rate of five feet per year, and water tables throughout India are falling an average of 3-10 feet per year.

Measures undertaken to increase water availability and to ease acute water shortages— using water more efficiently, expanding use of desalinization, developing genetically modified crops that use less water or more saline water, and importing water—will not be sufficient to substantially change the outlook for water shortages in 2015. Many will be expensive; policies to price water more realistically are not likely to be broadly implemented within the next 15 years, and subsidizing water is politically sensitive for the many low-income countries short of water because their populations expect cheap water.

Water has been a source of contention historically, but no water dispute has been a cause of open interstate conflict; indeed, water shortages often have stimulated cooperative arrangements for sharing the scarce resource. But as countries press against the limits of available water between now and 2015, the possibility of conflict will increase.

Nearly one-half of the world's land surface consists of river basins shared by more than one country, and more than 30 nations receive more than one-third of their water from outside their borders.

- Turkey is building new dams and irrigation projects on the Tigris and Euphrates Rivers, which will affect water flows into Syria and Iraq—two countries that will experience considerable population growth.

- Egypt is proceeding with a major diversion of water from the Nile, which flows from Ethiopia and Sudan, both of which will want to draw more water from the Nile for their own development by 2015. Water-sharing arrangements are likely to become more contentious.

Water shortages occurring in combination with other sources of tension—such as in the Middle East—will be the most worrisome.

Energy
The global economy will continue to become more energy efficient through 2015. Traditional industries, as well as transportation, are increasingly efficient in their energy use. Moreover, the most dynamic growth areas in the global economy, especially services and the knowledge fields, are less energy intensive than the economic activities that they replace. Energy production also is becoming more efficient. Technological applications, particularly in deep-water exploration and production, are opening remote and hostile areas to petroleum production.

Sustained global economic growth, along with population increases, will drive a nearly 50 percent increase in the demand for energy over the next 15 years. Total oil demand will increase from roughly 75 million barrels per day in 2000 to more than 100 million barrels in 2015, an increase almost as large as OPEC's current production. Over the next 15 years, natural gas usage will increase more rapidly than that of any other energy source—by more than 100 percent—mainly stemming from the tripling of gas consumption in Asia.

Asia will drive the expansion in energy demand, replacing North America as the leading energy consumption region and accounting for more than half of the world's total increase in demand.

- China, and to a lesser extent India, will see especially dramatic increases in energy consumption.

- By 2015, only one-tenth of Persian Gulf oil will be directed to Western markets; three-quarters will go to Asia.

Fossil fuels will remain the dominant form of energy despite increasing concerns about global warming. Efficiency of solar cells will improve, genetic engineering will increase the long-term prospects for the large-scale use of ethanol, and hydrates will be used increasingly as fuels. Nuclear energy use will remain at current levels.

Meeting the increase in demand for energy will pose neither a major supply challenge nor lead to substantial price increases in real terms. Estimates of the world's total endowment of oil have steadily increased as technological progress in extracting oil from remote sources has enabled new discoveries and more efficient production. Recent estimates indicate that 80 percent of the world's available oil still remains in the ground, as does 95 percent of the world's natural gas.

World Water Availability

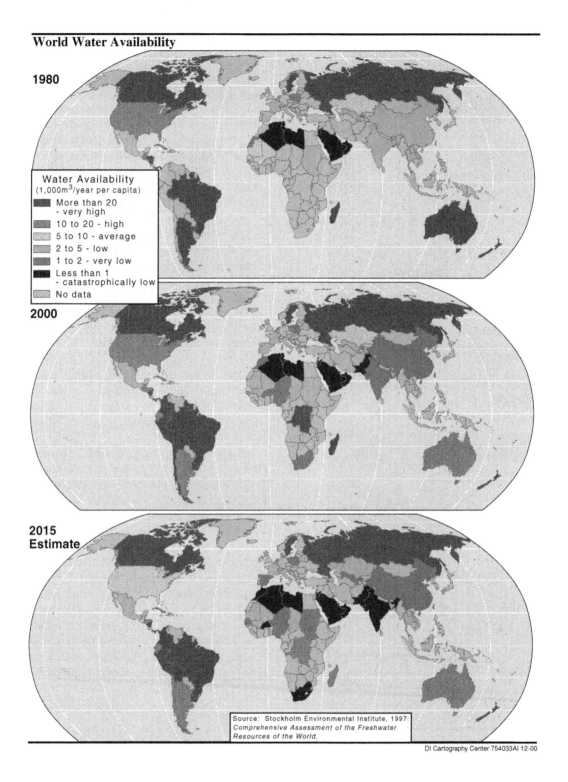

1980

Water Availability
(1,000m³/year per capita)

- More than 20 - very high
- 10 to 20 - high
- 5 to 10 - average
- 2 to 5 - low
- 1 to 2 - very low
- Less than 1 - catastrophically low
- No data

2000

2015 Estimate

Source: Stockholm Environmental Institute, 1997: *Comprehensive Assessment of the Freshwater Resources of the World.*

DI Cartography Center 754033AI 12-00

World Energy Consumption: 1970-2015

World Energy Consumption

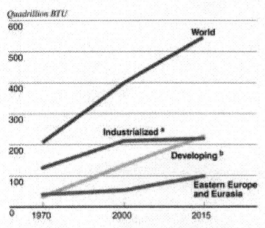

Quadrillion BTU

a Includes: United States, Canada, Mexico, Japan, United Kingdom, France, Germany, Italy, Netherlands, other Europe, and Australia.

b Includes: Developing Asia (China, India, South Korea, other Asia), Turkey, Africa, Brazil).

World Energy Consumption by Fuel Type

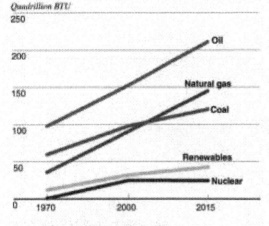

Quadrillion BTU

Source: International Energy Outlook, 1998; US Department of Energy.

DI Design Center 375950AI 10-00

- The Persian Gulf region—absent a major war—will see large increases in oil production capacity and will rise in its overall importance to the world energy market. Other areas of the world—including Russia, coastal West Africa, and Greenland—will also increase their role in global energy markets. Russia and the Middle East account for three-quarters of known gas reserves.

- Latin America—principally Venezuela, Mexico, and Brazil—has more than 117 billion barrels of proven oil reserves and potentially 114 billion barrels of undiscovered oil, according to the US Geological Survey. With foreign participation, Latin American production could increase from 9 million barrels per day to more than 14 million.

- Caspian energy development is likely to be in high gear by 2015. New transport routes for Caspian oil and gas exports that do not transit Russia will be operating.

Oil-producing countries will continue to exert leverage on the market to increase prices but are unlikely to achieve stable high prices. Energy prices are likely to become more unstable in the next 15 years, as periodic price hikes are followed by price collapses.

By 2015, global energy markets will have coalesced into two quasi-hemispheric patterns. Asia's energy needs will be met either through coal from the region or from oil and gas supplies from the Persian Gulf, Central Asia, and Russia. Western Europe and the Western Hemisphere will draw on the Atlantic Basin for their energy sources at world prices.

Environment

Contemporary environmental problems will persist and in many instances grow over the next 15 years. With increasingly intensive land use, significant degradation of arable land will continue as will the loss of tropical forests. Given the promising global economic outlook, greenhouse gas emissions will increase substantially. The depletion of tropical forests and other species-rich habitats, such as wetlands and coral reefs, will exacerbate the historically large losses of biological species now occurring.

- Environmental issues will become mainstream issues in several countries, particularly in the developed world. The consensus on the need to deal with environmental issues will strengthen; however, progress in dealing with them will be uneven.

The outlook to 2015 is mixed for such localized environmental problems as high concentrations of ozone and noxious chemicals in the air and the pollution of rivers and lakes by industrial and agricultural wastes.

- Developed countries will continue to manage these local environmental issues, and such issues are unlikely to constitute a major constraint on economic growth or on improving health standards.

- The developing countries, however, will face intensified environmental problems as a result of population growth, economic development, and rapid urbanization. An increasing number of cities will face the serious air and water quality problems that already are troubling in such urban centers as Mexico City, Sao Paulo, Lagos, and Beijing.

- Russia and Ukraine will struggle with problems stemming from decades of environmental neglect and abuse, including widespread radioactive pollution from badly managed nuclear facilities. These problems are unlikely to be adequately addressed. As these countries pursue economic growth, they will devote insufficient resources to environmental remediation.

- Central and Eastern European countries face similar problems as a result of the legacy of environmental neglect from the Communist era; nevertheless, driven by their desire to gain EU membership, several will become more effective in addressing these problems and will upgrade their environmental standards.

Some existing agreements, even when implemented, will not be able by 2015 to reverse the targeted environmental damage they were designed to address. The Montreal Protocol is on track to restore the stratospheric ozone layer over the next 50 years. Nevertheless, the seasonal Antarctic ozone hole will expand for the next two decades—increasing the risk of skin cancer in countries like Australia, Argentina, and Chile—because of the long lag time between emission reductions and atmospheric effects. Important new agreements will be implemented, including, for example, a global treaty to control the worldwide spread of such persistent organic chemicals as DDT and dioxins. Other agreements, such as the Convention on Biodiversity, will fall short in meeting their objectives.

Over the next 15 years the pressures on the environment as a result of economic growth will decrease as a result of less energy-intensive economic development and technological advances. For example, increased use of fuel cells and hybrid engines is likely to reduce the rate of increase in the amount of pollution produced, particularly in the transportation sector. Also, increases in the utilization of solar and wind power, advances in the efficiency of energy use, and a shift toward less polluting fuels, such as natural gas, will contribute to this trend.

Global warming will challenge the international community as indications of a warming climate—such as meltbacks of polar ice, sea level rise, and increasing frequency of major storms—occur. The Kyoto Protocol on Climate Change, which mandates emission-reduction targets for developed countries, is unlikely to come into force soon or without substantial modification. Even in the absence of a formal treaty, however, some incremental progress will be made in reducing the growth of greenhouse gas emissions.

- Both India and China will actively explore less carbon-intensive development strategies, although they will resist setting targets or timetables for carbon dioxide emission limits.

- A number of major firms operating internationally will take steps to reduce greenhouse gas emissions.

Science and Technology

The continuing diffusion of information technology and new applications in the biotechnology field will be of particular global significance. Two major trends will continue:

- *The integration of existing disciplines to form new ones*. The integration of information technology, biotechnology, materials sciences, and nanotechnology will generate a dramatic increase in innovation. The effects will be profound on business and commerce, public health, and safety.

- *The lateral development of technology*. Older established technologies will continue "sidewise" development into new markets and applications, for example, developing innovative applications for "old" computer chips.

The time between the discovery and the application of scientific advances will continue to shorten. Developments in the laboratory will reach commercial production at ever faster rates, leading to increased investments.

Information Technology (IT)

Over the next 15 years, a wide range of developments will lead to many new IT-enabled devices and services. Rapid diffusion is likely because equipment costs will decrease at the same time that demand is increasing. Local-to-global Internet access holds the prospect of universal wireless connectivity via hand-held devices and large numbers of low-cost, low-altitude satellites. Satellite systems and services will develop in ways that increase performance and reduce costs.

By 2015, information technology will make major inroads in rural as well as urban areas around the globe. Moreover, information technology need not be widespread to produce important effects. The first information technology "pioneers" in each society will be the local economic and political elites, multiplying the initial impact.

- Some countries and populations, however, will fail to benefit much from the information revolution.

- Among developing countries, India will remain in the forefront in developing information technology, led by the growing class of high-tech workers and entrepreneurs.

- China will lead the developing world in utilizing information technology, with urban areas leading the countryside. Beijing's capacity to control or shape the content of information, however, is likely to be sharply reduced.

- Although most Russian urban-dwellers will adopt information technologies well before 2015, the adoption of such technologies will be slow in the broader population.

- Latin America's Internet market will grow exponentially. Argentina, Mexico, and Brazil will accrue the greatest benefits because of larger telecommunications companies, bigger markets, and more international investment.

- In Sub-Saharan Africa, South Africa is best positioned to make relatively rapid progress in IT.

Societies with advanced communications generally will worry about threats to individual privacy. Others will worry about the spread of "cultural contamination." Governments everywhere will be simultaneously asked to foster the diffusion of IT while controlling its "harmful" effects.

Biotechnology

By 2015, the biotechnology revolution will be in full swing with major achievements in combating disease, increasing food production, reducing pollution, and enhancing the quality of life. Many of these developments, especially in the medical field, will remain costly through 2015 and will be available mainly in the West and to wealthy segments of other societies. Some biotechnologies will continue to be controversial for moral and religious reasons. Among the most significant developments by 2015 are:

- *Genomic profiling*—by decoding the genetic basis for pathology—will enable the medical community to move beyond the description of diseases to more effective mechanisms for diagnosis and treatment.

- *Biomedical engineering*, exploiting advances in biotechnology and "smart" materials, will produce new surgical procedures and systems, including better organic and artificial replacement parts for human beings, and the use of unspecialized human cells (stem cells) to augment or replace brain or body functions and structures. It also will spur development of sensor and neural prosthetics such as retinal implants for the eye, cochlear implants for the ear, or bypasses of spinal and other nerve damage.

- *Therapy and drug developments* will cure some enduring diseases and counter trends in antibiotic resistance. Deeper understanding of how particular diseases affect people with specific genetic characteristics will facilitate the development and prescription of custom drugs.

- *Genetic modification*—despite continuing technological and cultural barriers—will improve the engineering of organisms to increase food production and quality, broaden the scale of bio-manufacturing, and provide cures for certain genetic diseases. Cloning will be used for such applications as livestock production. Despite cultural and political concerns, the use of genetically modified crops has great potential to dramatically improve the nutrition and health of many of the world's poorest people.

- *DNA identification* will continue to improve law enforcement capabilities.

Other Technologies

Breakthroughs in **materials technology** will generate widely available products that are smart, multifunctional, environmentally compatible, more survivable, and customizable. These products not only will contribute to the growing information and biotechnology revolutions but also will benefit manufacturing, logistics, and personal lifestyles. Materials with active capabilities will be used to combine sensing and actuation in response to environmental conditions.

Discoveries in **nanotechnology** will lead to unprecedented understanding and control over the fundamental building blocks of all physical things. Developments in this emerging field are likely to change the way almost everything—from vaccines to computers to automobile tires to objects not yet imagined—is designed and made. Self-assembled nanomaterials, such as semiconductor "quantum dots," could by 2015 revolutionize chemical labeling and enable rapid processing for drug discovery, blood content analysis, genetic analysis, and other biological applications.

The Global Economy

The global economy is well-positioned to achieve a sustained period of dynamism through 2015. Global economic growth will return to the high levels reached in the 1960s and early 1970s, the final years of the post-World War II "long boom." Dynamism will be strongest among so-called "emerging markets"—especially in the two Asian giants, China and India—but will be broadly based worldwide, including in both industrialized and many developing countries. The rising tide of the global economy will create many economic winners, but it will not lift all boats. The information revolution will make the persistence of poverty more visible, and regional differences will remain large.

Dynamism and Growth

Five factors will combine to promote widespread economic dynamism and growth:

Political pressures for higher living standards. The growing global middle class—now 2 billion strong—is creating a cycle of rising aspirations, with increased information flows and the spread of democracy giving political clout to formerly disenfranchised citizens.

Improved macroeconomic policies. The widespread improvement in recent years in economic policy and management sets the stage for future dynamism. Inflation rates have been dramatically lowered across a wide range of economies. The abandonment of unsustainable fixed exchange rate regimes in Asia and the creation of the European Monetary Union (EMU) will contribute to economic growth.

Rising trade and investment. International trade and investment flows will grow, spurring rapid increases in world GDP. Opposition to further trade liberalization from special interest groups and some governments will not erode the basic trend toward expansion of trade. International capital flows, which have risen dramatically in the past decade, will remain plentiful, especially for emerging market countries that increase their transparency.

Diffusion of information technology. The pervasive incorporation of information technologies will continue to produce significant efficiency gains in the US economy. Similar gains will be witnessed—albeit in varying degrees—in numerous other countries as the

Regional GDP: 1970-2015

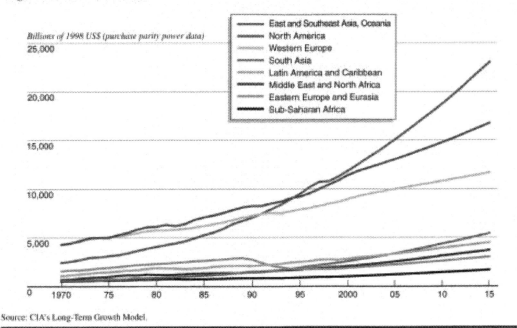

Billions of 1998 US$ (purchase parity power data)

Legend:
- East and Southeast Asia, Oceania
- North America
- Western Europe
- South Asia
- Latin America and Caribbean
- Middle East and North Africa
- Eastern Europe and Eurasia
- Sub-Saharan Africa

Source: CIA's Long-Term Growth Model.

DI Design Center 375953AI 10-00

integration of these technologies proceeds. But the absorption of IT and its benefits will not be automatic because many countries will fail to meet the conditions needed for effective IT utilization—high educational levels, adequate infrastructure, and appropriate regulatory policies.

Increasingly dynamic private sectors. Rapid expansion of the private sector in many emerging market countries—along with deregulation and privatization in Europe and Japan—will spur economic growth by generating competitive pressures to use resources more efficiently. The impact of improved efficiencies will be multiplied as the information revolution enhances the ability of firms around the world to learn "best practices" from the most successful enterprises. Indeed, the world may be on the verge of a rapid convergence in market-based financial and business practices.

Unequal Growth Prospects and Distribution
The countries and regions most at risk of falling behind economically are those with endemic internal and/or regional conflicts and those that fail to diversify their economies. The economies of most states in Sub-Saharan Africa and the Middle East and some in Latin America will continue to suffer. A large segment of the Eurasian landmass extending from Central Asia through the Caucasus to parts of southeastern Europe faces dim economic prospects. Within countries, the gap in the standard of living also will increase. Even in rapidly growing countries, large regions will be left behind.

World Trade as a Percentage of World GDP: 1990-2015

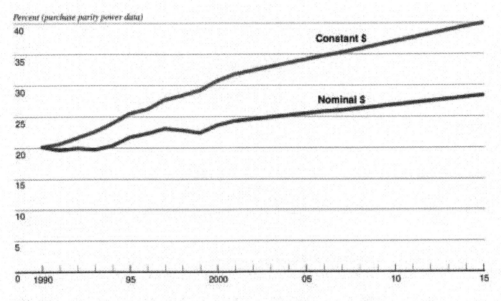

Percent (purchase parity power data)

Constant $

Nominal $

NOTE: The constant dollar curve departs from the nominal curve largely because of the fall in price of IT-related traded goods in the 1990s and their expected price decline in the future.

Source: CIA's Long-Term Growth Model.

DI Design Center 375952N 10-00

Emerging Asia will be the fastest growing region, led by breakout candidates China and India, whose economies already comprise roughly one-sixth of global GDP. To the degree that China implements reforms mandated by its entry into the World Trade Organization, its economy will become more efficient, enabling rapid growth to continue. China's economic development, however, will be mainly in the dynamic coastal provinces. Agricultural provinces in northern and western China will lag behind, causing social tensions that Beijing will be challenged to manage. India's relatively strong educational system, democracy, and English-language skills position it well to take advantage of gains related to information technology. India nevertheless faces enormous challenges in spreading the benefits of growth to hundreds of millions of impoverished, often illiterate citizens, particularly in the northern states.

In Europe and Japan, the picture is mixed. **Western Europe** is likely to narrow what has been a growing economic performance gap with the United States, and **Eastern European** countries, eager for EU membership, generally will adopt reform policies and grow apace. **South-Eastern Europe** will improve economic prospects only gradually as it improves regional security. Although **Japan's** economic performance in the next 15 years will be

Regional GDP: 1970-2015

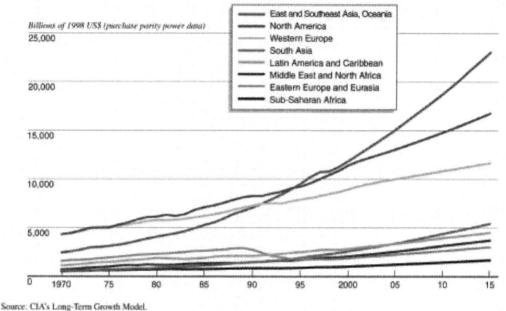

Billions of 1998 US$ (purchase parity power data)

Legend:
- East and Southeast Asia, Oceania
- North America
- Western Europe
- South Asia
- Latin America and Caribbean
- Middle East and North Africa
- Eastern Europe and Eurasia
- Sub-Saharan Africa

Y-axis: 25,000 / 20,000 / 15,000 / 10,000 / 5,000 / 0

X-axis: 1970 / 75 / 80 / 85 / 90 / 95 / 2000 / 05 / 10 / 15

Source: CIA's Long-Term Growth Model.

DI Design Center 375953AI 10-00

stronger than that of the 1990s, its relative importance in the global economy will decrease. Economic prospects for **Russia and Eurasia** are not promising.

Latin America will manage fairly rapid aggregate growth, but it will be spread unevenly across the region. The market-oriented democracies in Mexico and the southern cone will lead the way. A new generation of entrepreneurs will be inclined to favor additional market openings, but the benefits may further distort income distribution, already the most inequitable in the world. Elsewhere, the Andean region will struggle with a poorly educated labor force, unstable governance, and dependence upon commodities such as oil, copper, and narcotics.

The Middle East and North Africa will be marked by increasing internal differentiation as some countries respond more effectively to the challenges of globalization or to the uncertainties of closer integration with the EU while others lag. In **Sub-Saharan Africa**, persistent conflicts and instability, autocratic and corrupt governments, overdependence on commodities with declining real prices, low levels of education, and widespread infectious diseases will combine to prevent most countries from experiencing rapid economic growth.

37

Economic Crises and Resilience

The global economy will be prone to periodic financial crises, but its capacity to correct itself will remain strong. The rapid rebound from the global financial crisis of 1997-98, the limited impact of the recent tripling of oil prices on global economic growth, and the successful management of the "Y2K" problem are the most recent manifestations of resilience. Nonetheless, economic liberalization and globalization entail risks and inevitably will create bumps in the road, some of them potentially highly disruptive.

- *Economic crises will recur*. The trends toward free markets and deregulation will allow financial markets to overshoot, increase the possibility for sudden reversal in sentiment, and expose individual countries to broad swings in the global market. Any of these could trigger a financial crisis.

- *Turbulence in one economy will affect others*. Increased trade links and the integration of global financial markets will quickly transmit turmoil in one economy regionally and internationally, as Russia's financial turmoil in 1998 affected Brazil.

- *Disputes over international economic rules*. The Asian financial crisis revealed differences among countries regarding global financial architecture. As emerging market countries continue to grow, they will seek a stronger voice in setting the terms of international economic governance. A lack of consensus could at times make financial markets skittish and undermine growth.

National and International Governance

The state will remain the single most important organizing unit of political, economic, and security affairs through 2015 but will confront fundamental tests of effective governance. The first will be to benefit from, while coping with, several facets of globalization. The second will be to deal with increasingly vocal and organized publics.

- The elements of globalization—greater and freer flow of information, capital, goods, services, people, and the diffusion of power to nonstate actors of all kinds—will challenge the authority of virtually all governments. At the same time, globalization will create demands for increased international cooperation on transnational issues.

38

Alternative Trajectories

Although the outlook for the global economy appears quite strong, achieving sustained high levels of global growth will be contingent on avoiding several potential brakes to growth. Five are described below.

The US economy suffers a sustained downturn. Given the large trade deficit and low domestic savings, the US economy—the most important driver of recent global growth—is vulnerable to loss of international confidence in its growth prospects that could lead to a sharp downturn, which, if long-lasting, would have deleterious economic and policy consequences for the rest of the world. Key trading partners would suffer as the world's largest market contracted, and international financial markets might face profound instability.

Europe and Japan fail to manage their demographic challenges. European and Japanese populations are aging rapidly, requiring more than 110 million new workers by 2015 to maintain current dependency ratios between the working population and retirees. For these countries, immigration is a controversial means of meeting these labor force requirements. Conflicts over the social contract or immigration policies in major European states could dampen economic growth. Japan faces an even more serious labor force shortage and its strategies for responding— enticing overseas Japanese to return, broadening the opportunities for women, and increasing investments elsewhere in Asia— may prove inadequate. If growth in Europe and Japan falters, the economic burden on the US economy would increase, weakening the overall global outlook.

China and/or India fail to sustain high growth. China's ambitious goals for reforming its economy will be difficult to realize: restructuring state-owned enterprises, cleaning up and transforming the banking system, cutting the government's employment rolls in half, and opening up the economy to greater foreign competition. Growth would slow if these reforms go awry, which, in turn, would exacerbate bureaucratic wrangling and increase opposition to the reform agenda. India's reform drive—essential to sustained economic growth—could be sidetracked by social divisions and by the bureaucratic culture of the public service.

Emerging market countries fail to reform their financial institutions. Although most emerging market countries bounced back from the 1997-98 financial crisis more quickly than expected, many have not yet undertaken the financial reforms needed to help them survive the next economic crisis. Absent such reform, a series of future economic crises in emerging market countries could dry up the capital flows crucial for high rates of economic growth.

Global energy supplies are disrupted in a major way. Although the world economy is less vulnerable to energy price swings than in the 1970s, a major disruption in global energy supplies still would have a devastating effect. Conflict among key energy-producing states, sustained internal instability in two or more major energy-producing states, or major terrorist actions could lead to such a disruption.

- All states will confront popular demands for greater participation in politics and attention to civil rights—pressures that will encourage greater democratization and transparency. Twenty-five years ago less than a third of states were defined as democracies by Freedom House; today more than half of states are considered democracies, albeit with varying combinations of electoral and civil or political rights. The majority of states are likely to remain democracies in some sense over the next 15 years, but the number of new democracies that are likely to develop is uncertain.

Successful states will interact with nonstate actors to manage authority and share responsibility. Between now and 2015, three important challenges for states will be:

- Managing relations with nonstate actors;

- Combating criminal networks; and

- Responding to emerging and dynamic religious and ethnic groups.

Nonstate Actors

States continually will be dealing with private-sector organizations—both for-profit and nonprofit. These nonstate actors increasingly will gain resources and power over the next 15 years as a result of the ongoing liberalization of global finance and trade, as well as the opportunities afforded by information technology.

The For-profit Sector. The for-profit business sector will grow rapidly over the next 15 years, spearheading legal and judicial reform and challenging governments to become more transparent and predictable. At the same time, governments will be challenged to monitor and regulate business firms through measures consistent with local standards of social welfare.

Multinational corporations—now numbering more than 50,000 with nearly one-half million affiliates—have multiplied in recent years as governments have deregulated their economies, privatized state-owned enterprises, and liberalized financial markets and trade. This trend will continue.

Medium-sized, mostly local firms will multiply in many countries, driven by the shift away from Communism and other socialist models and the broadening of financial services and banking systems. Micro-enterprises also will multiply, not only because of deregulation and liberalization, but also because many states will have a declining capacity to stymie small-scale commercial activities. As medium-sized and small businesses become more numerous, they will encourage, and then link into, various global networks.

The Nonprofit Sector. Nonprofit networks with affiliates in more than one country will grow through 2015, having expanded more than 20-fold between 1964 and 1998. Within individual countries, the nonprofit sector also will expand rapidly.

Over the next 15 years international and national nonprofits will not only expand but change in significant ways.

- Nonprofit organizations will have more resources to expand their activities and will become more confident of their power and more confrontational. Nonprofits will move beyond delivering services to the design and implementation of policies, whether as partners or competitors with corporations and governments.

- Western preponderance will persist but at a declining level as economic growth in Asia and Latin America produces additional resources for support of civil society. In addition, autocratic governments and Islamic states or groups will increasingly support nonprofit groups sympathetic to their interests.

- Nonprofit organizations will be expected to meet codes of conduct. Governments and corporations—which are increasingly held to standards of transparency and accountability—will, in turn, expect nonprofits to meet similar standards.

Criminal Organizations and Networks

Over the next 15 years, transnational criminal organizations will become increasingly adept at exploiting the global diffusion of sophisticated information, financial, and transportation networks.

Criminal organizations and networks based in North America, Western Europe, China, Colombia, Israel, Japan, Mexico, Nigeria, and Russia will expand the scale and scope of their activities. They will form loose alliances with one another, with smaller criminal entrepreneurs, and with insurgent movements for specific operations. They will corrupt leaders of unstable, economically fragile or failing states, insinuate themselves into troubled banks and businesses, and cooperate with insurgent political movements to control substantial geographic areas. Their income will come from narcotics trafficking; alien smuggling; trafficking in women and children; smuggling toxic materials, hazardous wastes, illicit arms, military technologies, and other contraband; financial fraud; and racketeering.

- The risk will increase that organized criminal groups will traffic in nuclear, biological, or chemical weapons. The degree of risk depends on whether governments with WMD capabilities can or will control such weapons and materials.

Changing Communal Identities and Networks

Traditional communal groups—whether religious or ethnic-linguistic groups—will pose a range of challenges for governance. Using opportunities afforded by globalization and the opening of civil society, communal groups will be better positioned to mobilize coreligionists or ethnic kin to assert their interests or defend against perceived economic or political discrimination. Ethnic diasporas and coreligionists abroad also will be more able and willing to provide fraternal groups with political, financial, and other support.

An effective combination of high tech and criminal activity: a stolen Mercedes loaded onto a fast getaway boat. Criminal networks will take advantage of new technologies to facilitate activities and expand operations.

DI Design Center 375588AI 10-00

Estimates of the number of distinct ethnic-linguistic groups at the beginning of the twenty-first century run from 2,000 to 5,000, ranging from small bands living in isolated areas to larger groups living in ancestral homelands or in diasporas. Most of the world's 191 states are ethnically heterogeneous, and many contain ethnic populations with co-ethnics in neighboring states. By 2015, ethnic heterogeneity will increase in almost all states, as a result of international migration and divergent birthrates of migrant and native populations.

Communal tensions, sometimes culminating in conflict, probably will increase through 2015. In addition to some ongoing communal frictions that will persist, triggers of new tensions will include:

- **Repression by the state.** States with slow economic growth, and/or where executive power is concentrated in an exclusionary political elite and the rule of law and civil or minority rights are weak, will be inclined to

- By 2015, Christianity and Islam, the two largest religious groupings, will have grown significantly. Both are widely dispersed in several continents, already use information technologies to "spread the faith," and draw on adherents to fund numerous nonprofit groups and political causes. Activist components of these and other religious groupings will emerge to contest such issues as genetic manipulation, women's rights, and the income gap between rich and poor. A wider religious or spiritual movement also may emerge, possibly linked to environmental values.

Current World Illicit Trafficking

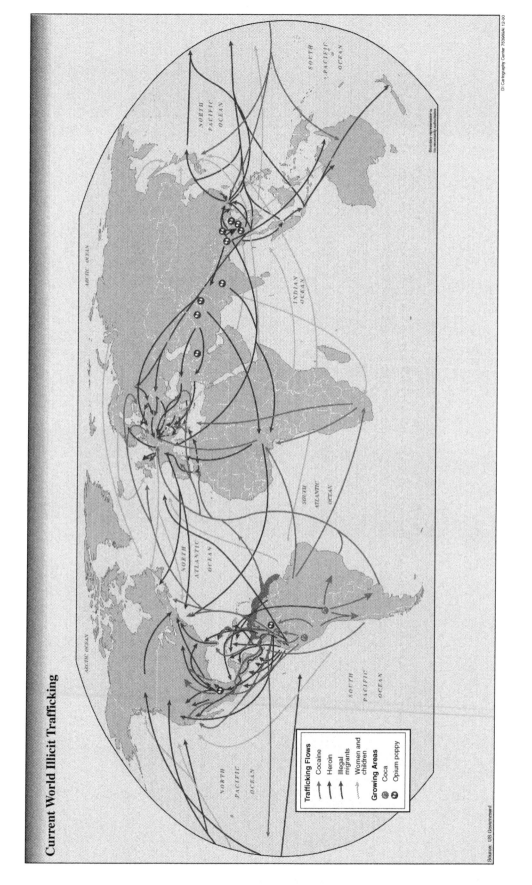

Trafficking Flows
- Cocaine
- Heroin
- Illegal migrants
- Women and children

Growing Areas
- Coca
- Opium poppy

Boundary representation is not necessarily authoritative.

DI Cartography Center 753966A4 12-00

Worldwide Adherents of Selected Major Religions, Mid-1998

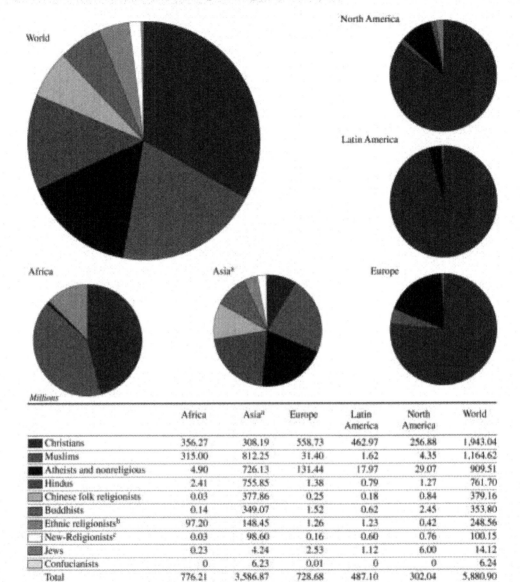

Millions

	Africa	Asia[a]	Europe	Latin America	North America	World
Christians	356.27	308.19	558.73	462.97	256.88	1,943.04
Muslims	315.00	812.25	31.40	1.62	4.35	1,164.62
Atheists and nonreligious	4.90	726.13	131.44	17.97	29.07	909.51
Hindus	2.41	755.85	1.38	0.79	1.27	761.70
Chinese folk religionists	0.03	377.86	0.25	0.18	0.84	379.16
Buddhists	0.14	349.07	1.52	0.62	2.45	353.80
Ethnic religionists[b]	97.20	148.45	1.26	1.23	0.42	248.56
New-Religionists[c]	0.03	98.60	0.16	0.60	0.76	100.15
Jews	0.23	4.24	2.53	1.12	6.00	14.12
Confucianists	0	6.23	0.01	0	0	6.24
Total	776.21	3,586.87	728.68	487.10	302.04	5,880.90

Source: Encyclopedia Britannica World Book, 1999.

[a] Asia includes Middle East and Central Asia.

[b] Followers of local tribal, animalistic, or shamanistic religions.

[c] Followers of primarily crisis or syncretistic religions and movements, all founded since 1800 and most since 1995.

discriminate against communal minorities. Such conditions will foment ethnic tensions in Sub-Saharan Africa, Central and South Asia, and parts of the Middle East, often in rapidly growing urban areas. Certain powerful states—such as Russia, China, Brazil, and India—also are likely to repress politicized communal minorities.

- *Religious, often fused with ethnic, grievances*. Few Muslim states will grant full political and cultural rights to religious minorities. At the same time, they will not remain indifferent to the treatment of Muslim minorities elsewhere: in Russia, Indonesia, India/Kashmir, China, and the Balkans. Other religious denominations also will support beleaguered coreligionists.

- *Resistance to migration*. Some relatively homogenous countries or sub-regions in Asia and Europe will resist ethnically diverse migrants, creating tensions.

- *Indigenous protest movements*. Such movements will increase, facilitated by transnational networks of indigenous rights activists and supported by well-funded international human rights and environmental groups. Tensions will intensify in the area from Mexico through the Amazon region; northeastern India; and the Malaysian-Indonesian archipelago.

Overall Impact on States
The developed democracies will be best positioned for good governance because they will tend to empower legitimate nonstate actors in both the for-profit and nonprofit sectors; will favor institutions and processes that accommodate divergent communal groups; will press for transparency in government and the efficient delivery of public services; and will maintain institutions to regulate legitimate for-profit and nonprofit organizations and control illegitimate criminal groups. Countries in Western Europe, Canada, Australia, New Zealand, and Japan have the requisite agility and institutions to meet the challenges. Countries in Eastern Europe as well as Turkey, South Korea, India, Chile, and Brazil, among other developing countries, are moving in these directions, despite some continuing obstacles.

Some newly democratic states and modernizing authoritarian states will have leaders amenable to technological change and access to substantial human and financial resources. They will encourage business firms, nonprofits, and communal groups supportive of the government and discourage or suppress those that are independent-minded or critical of government policies. They will have some success in coping with the energy, ideas, and resources of nonstate actors. Several Asian countries, such as Singapore, Taiwan, and perhaps China, as well as some states in the Middle East and Latin America are likely to take this approach.

Other states in varying degrees will lack the resources and leadership to achieve effective governance. Most autocratic states in the Middle East and Africa will not have the institutions or cultural orientation to exploit the opportunities provided by nonstate actors— apart from certain forms of humanitarian assistance. In many of these countries, nonstate actors will become more important than governments in providing services, such as health clinics and schools. In the weakest of these countries, communal, criminal, or terrorist groups will seek control of government institutions and/or territory.

Overall, the number of states—which has more than tripled since 1945 and has grown 20 percent since 1990—is likely to increase at a slower rate through 2015. This growth will result from remaining cases of decolonization and to communal tensions leading to state secession, most likely in Sub-Saharan Africa, Central Asia, and Indonesia. In some cases, new states will inspire other secessionist movements, destabilizing countries where minorities were not initially seeking secession.

At the same time, the very concept of "belonging" to a particular state probably will erode among a growing number of people with continuing transnational ties to more than one country through citizenship, residence or other associations.

International Cooperation

Globalization and technological change are raising widespread expectations that increased international cooperation will help manage many transnational problems that states can no longer manage on their own. Efforts to realize such expectations will increase, but concerns about national interests as well as the costs and risks involved in some types of international activism will limit success.

Mechanisms of international cooperation—intended to facilitate bargaining, elucidate common interests and resolve differences among states—have increased rapidly in recent decades.

- International treaties registered with the United Nations more than tripled between 1970 and 1997. In addition, there are growing numbers of agreements on standards and practices initiated by self-selected private networks.

- The number of international institutions increased by two-thirds from 1985 until 1999, while at the same time becoming more complex, more interrelated with often overlapping areas of responsibility, and more closely linked to transnational networks and private groups.

International cooperation will continue to increase through 2015, particularly when large economic stakes have mobilized the for-profit sector, and/or when there is intense interest from nonprofit groups and networks.

Most high-income democratic states will participate in multiple international institutions and seek cooperation on a wide range of issues to protect their interests and to promote their influence. Members of the European Union will tackle the most ambitious agenda, including significant political and security cooperation.

Strongly nationalistic and/or autocratic states will play selective roles in inter-governmental organizations: working within them to protect and project their interests, while working against initiatives that they view as threatening to their domestic power structures and national sovereignty. They will also work against those international institutions viewed as creatures of the established great powers and thus rigged against them—such as the IMF and the WTO—as well as those that cede a major role to non-state actors.

Low-income developing countries will participate actively in international organizations and arrangements to assert their sovereignty, garner resources for social and economic development, and gain support for the incumbent government. The most unstable of these states will participate in international organizations and arrangements primarily to maintain international recognition for the regime.

Agenda for International Cooperation

Cooperation is likely to be effective in such areas as:

• Monitoring international financial flows and financial safehavens.

• Law enforcement against corruption, and against trafficking in narcotics and women and children.

• Monitoring meteorological data and warning of extreme weather events.

• Selected environmental issues, such as reducing substances that deplete the ozone layer or conserving high-seas fisheries.

• Developing vaccines or medicines against major infectious diseases, such as HIV/AIDS or malaria and surveillance of infectious disease outbreaks.

• Humanitarian assistance for refugees and for victims of famines, natural disasters, and internal conflicts where relief organizations can gain access.

• Counterterrorism.

• Efforts by international and regional organizations to resolve some internal and interstate conflicts, particularly in Africa.

Cooperation is likely to be contentious and with mixed results in such areas as:

• Conditions under which Intellectual Property Rights are protected.

• Reform and strengthening of international financial institutions, particularly the Bretton Woods institutions.

• Expansion of the UN Security Council.

• Adherence by major states to an International Criminal Court with universal, comprehensive jurisdiction.

• Control of greenhouse gas emissions to reduce global warming, carrying out the purposes of the 1997 Kyoto Protocol on Climate Change.

• Acceptance of genetically-modified organisms to improve nutrition and health in poor regions.

• Establishing peacekeeping forces and standby military forces under the authority of the UN Security Council or most regional organizations, with the possible exception of the EU.

(continued)

Future Conflict

Through 2015, internal conflicts will pose the most frequent threat to stability around the world. Interstate wars, though less frequent, will grow in lethality due to the availability of more destructive technologies. The international community will have to deal with the military, political, and economic dimensions of the rise of China and India and the continued decline of Russia.

Internal Conflicts

Many internal conflicts, particularly those arising from communal disputes, will continue to be vicious, long-lasting and difficult to terminate—leaving bitter legacies in their wake.

• They frequently will spawn internal displacements, refugee flows, humanitarian emergencies, and other regionally destabilizing dislocations.

• If left to fester, internal conflicts will trigger spillover into inter-state conflicts as neighboring states move to exploit opportunities for gain or to limit the possibilities of damage to their national interests.

• Weak states will spawn recurrent internal conflicts, threatening the stability of a globalizing international system.

Internal conflicts stemming from state repression, religious and ethnic grievances, increasing migration pressures, and/or indigenous protest movements will occur most frequently in Sub-Saharan Africa, the Caucasus and Central Asia, and parts of south and southeast Asia, Central America and the Andean region.

The United Nations and several regional organizations will continue to be called upon to manage some internal conflicts because major states—stressed by domestic concerns, perceived risk of failure, lack of political will, or tight resources—will wish to minimize their direct involvement. When, however, some Western governments, international and regional organizations, and civil-society groups press for outside military intervention in certain internal conflicts, they will be opposed by such states as China, India, Russia and many developing countries that will tend to view interventions as dangerous precedents challenging state sovereignty.

Transnational Terrorism

States with poor governance; ethnic, cultural, or religious tensions; weak economies; and porous borders will be prime breeding grounds for terrorism. In such states, domestic groups will challenge the entrenched government, and transnational networks seeking safehavens.

At the same time, the trend away from state-supported political terrorism and toward more diverse, free-wheeling, transnational networks—enabled by information technology—will continue. Some of the states that actively sponsor terrorism or terrorist groups today may decrease or even cease their support by 2015 as a result of regime changes, rapprochement with neighbors, or the conclusion that terrorism has become counterproductive. But weak states also could drift toward cooperation with terrorists, creating defacto new state supporters.

• Between now and 2015 terrorist tactics will become increasingly sophisticated and designed to achieve mass casualties. We expect the trend toward greater lethality in terrorist attacks to continue.

Terrorists bombed the US Embassy in Nairobi, Kenya, in August 1998, leaving hundreds dead and wounded. International terrorists will still be active in 2015 and could become more lethal with the proliferation of more powerful high-tech weapons.

DI Design Center 379590AI 10-00

Interstate Conflicts

Over the next 15 years, the international system will have to adjust to changing power relationships in key regions:

• *China's potential*. Estimates of China beyond five years are fraught with unknowables. Some projections indicate that Chinese power will rise because of the growth of its economic and military capabilities. Other projections indicate that the array of political, social, and economic pressures will increasingly challenge the stability and legitimacy of the regime. Most assessments today argue that China will seek to avoid conflict in the region to promote stable economic growth and to ensure internal stability. A strong China, others assert, would seek to adjust regional power arrangements to its advantage, risking conflict with neighbors and some powers external to the region. A weak China would increase prospects for criminality, narcotics trafficking, illegal migration, WMD proliferation, and widespread social instability.

Current Ethnic Diversity of States

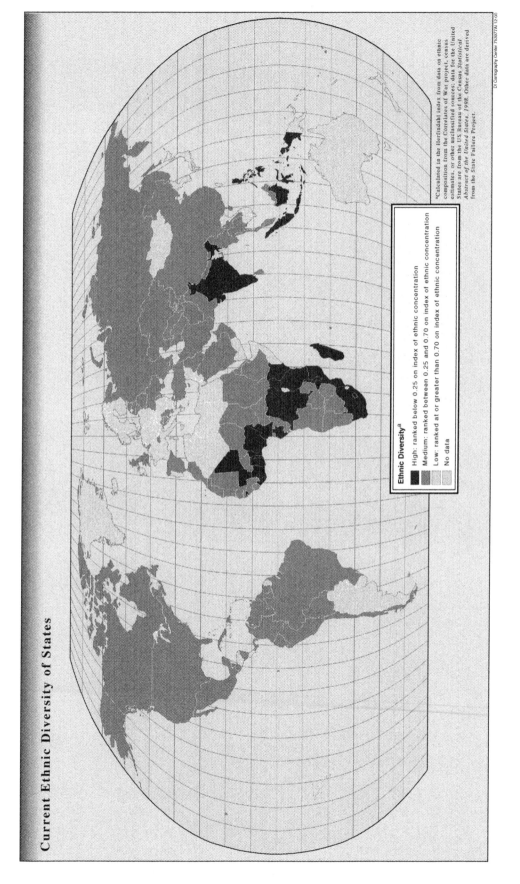

Ethnic Diversity[a]

■ High: ranked below 0.25 on index of ethnic concentration
▨ Medium: ranked between 0.25 and 0.70 on index of ethnic concentration
▤ Low: ranked at or greater than 0.70 on index of ethnic concentration
□ No data

[a]Calculated is the Herfindahl index from data on ethnic composition from the Correlates of War project, census estimates, or other unclassified sources; data for the United States are from the US Bureau of the Census Statistical Abstract of the United States, 1998. Other data are derived from the State Failure Project.

DI Cartography Center 753677A1 12-00

- *Russia's decline*. By 2015, Russia will be challenged even more than today to adjust its expectations for world leadership to the dramatically reduced resources it will have to play that role. The quality of Russian governance is an open question as is whether the country will be able to make the transition in a manner that preserves rather than upsets regional stability.

- *Japan's uncertainty*. In the view of many experts, Japan will have difficulty maintaining its current position as the world's third largest economy by 2015. Tokyo has so far not shown a willingness to carry through the painful economic reforms necessary to slow the erosion of its leadership role in Asia. In the absence of an external shock, Japan is similarly unlikely to accelerate changes in security policy.

- *India's prospects*. India will strengthen its role as a regional power, but many uncertainties about the effects of global trends on its society cast doubt on how far India will go. India faces growing extremes between wealth and poverty, a mixed picture on natural resources, and problems with internal governance.

The changing dynamics of state power will combine with other factors to affect the risk of conflict in various regions. Changing military capabilities will be prominent among the factors that determine the risk of war. In South Asia, for example, that risk will remain fairly high over the next 15 years. India and Pakistan are both prone to miscalculation. Both will continue to build up their nuclear and missile forces.

India most likely will expand the size of its nuclear-capable force. *Pakistan's* nuclear and missile forces also will continue to increase.

Islamabad has publicly claimed that the number of nuclear weapons and missiles it deploys will be based on "minimum" deterrence and will be independent of the size of India's arsenal. A noticeable increase in the size of India's arsenal, however, would prompt Pakistan to further increase the size of its own arsenal.

Russia will be unable to maintain conventional forces that are both sizable and modern or to project significant military power with conventional means. The Russian military will increasingly rely on its shrinking strategic and theater nuclear arsenals to deter or, if deterrence fails, to counter large-scale conventional assaults on Russian territory.

- Moscow will maintain as many strategic missiles and associated nuclear warheads as it believes it can afford but well short of START I or II limitations. The total Russian force by 2015, including air launched cruise missiles, probably will be below 2,500 warheads.

As Russia struggles with the constraints on its ambitions, it will invest scarce resources in selected and secretive military technology programs, especially WMD, hoping to counter Western conventional and strategic superiority in areas such as ballistic missile defense.

China's People's Liberation Army (PLA) will remain the world's largest military, but the majority of the force will not be fully modernized by 2015. China could close the technological gap with the West in one or more major weapons systems. China's capability for regional military operations is likely to improve significantly by 2015.

China: How to Think About Its Growing Wealth and Power

China has been riding the crest of a significant wave of economic growth for two decades. Many experts assess that China can maintain a growth rate of 7 percent or more for many years. Such impressive rates provide a foundation for military potential, and some predict that China's rapid economic growth will lead to a significant increase in military capabilities. But the degree to which an even more powerful economy would translate into greater military power is uncertain.

The relationship between economic growth and China's overall power will derive from the priorities of leaders in Beijing—provided the regime remains stable. China's leaders have assessed for some years that comprehensive national power derives both from economic strength and from the military and diplomatic resources that a healthy, large economy makes possible. They apparently agree that, for the foreseeable future, such priorities as agricultural and national infrastructure modernization must take precedence over military development. In the absence of a strong national security challenge, this view is unlikely to change even as new leaders emerge in Beijing. In a stable environment, two leadership transitions will occur in China between now and 2015. The

evidence strongly suggests that the new leaders will be even more firmly committed to developing the economy as the foundation of national power and that resources for military capabilities will take a secondary role. Existing priorities and projected defense allocations could enable the PLA to emerge as the most powerful regional military force.

• *Beyond resource issues, China faces daunting challenges in producing defense systems. Beijing has yet to demonstrate an assured capacity to translate increasingly sophisticated science and technology advances into first-rate military production. To achieve this, China must effect reforms in its State Owned Enterprises (SOEs), develop a capacity for advanced systems integration skills, and recruit and retain technologically sophisticated officers and enlisted personnel.*

A decision to alter priorities to emphasize military development would require substantial change in the leadership. Internal instability or a rise in nationalism could produce such change but also probably would result in economic decline.

• China will be exploiting advanced weapons and production technologies acquired from abroad—Russia, Israel, Europe, Japan, and the United States—that will enable it to integrate naval and air capabilities against Taiwan and potential adversaries in the South China Sea.

- In the event of a peaceful resolution of the Taiwan issue, some of China's military objectives—such as protecting the sea lanes for Persian Gulf oil—could become more congruent with those of the United States. Nevertheless, as an emerging regional power, China would continue to expand its influence without regard to US interests.

- China by 2015 will have deployed tens to several tens of missiles with nuclear warheads targeted against the United States, mostly more survivable land- and sea-based mobile missiles. It also will have hundreds of shorter-range ballistic and cruise missiles for use in regional conflicts. Some of these shorter-range missiles will have nuclear warheads; most will be armed with conventional warheads.

Japan has a small but modern military force, more able than any other in Asia to integrate large quantities of new weaponry. Japan's future military strength will reflect the state of its economy and the health of its security relationship with the United States. Tokyo will increasingly pursue greater autonomy in security matters and develop security enhancements, such as defense improvements and more active diplomacy, to supplement the US alliance.

A unified Korea with a significant US military presence may become a regional military power. For the next 10 to 15 years, however, knowledgeable observers suggest that the process of unification will consume *South Korea's* energies and resources.

Absent unification, *North Korea's* WMD capabilities will continue to cloud regional stability. P'yongyang probably has one, possibly two, nuclear weapons. It has developed medium-range missiles for years and has tested a three-stage space launch vehicle.

P'yonyang may improve the accuracy, range, and payload capabilities of its Taepo Dong-2 ICBM, deploy variants, or develop more capable systems. North Korea could have a few to several Taepo Dong-2 type missiles deployed by 2005.

In the *Middle East*, the confluence of domestic economic pressures and regional rivalries is likely to further the proliferation of weapons of mass destruction and the means to deliver them. By contrast, spending on conventional arms probably will remain stable or decline in most countries. Some governments may maintain large armed forces to absorb otherwise unemployable youths, but such armies will be less well trained and equipped. Rather than conventional war, the region is likely to experience more terrorism, insurgencies, and humanitarian emergencies arising from internal disparities or disputes over ethnic or religious identity.

- *Iran* sees its short- and medium-range missiles as deterrents, as force-multiplying weapons of war, primarily with conventional warheads, and as options for delivering biological, chemical, and eventually nuclear weapons. Iran could test an IRBM or land-attack cruise missile by 2004 and perhaps even an ICBM or space launch vehicle as early as 2001.

- *Iraq's* ability to obtain WMD will be influenced, in part, by the degree to which the UN Security Council can impede development or procurement over the next 15 years. Under some scenarios, Iraq could test an ICBM capable of delivering nuclear-sized payloads to the United States before 2015; foreign assistance would affect the capabilities of the missile and the time it became available. Iraq could also develop a nuclear weapon during this period.

Reacting to US Military Superiority
Experts agree that the United States, with its decisive edge in both information and weapons technology, will remain the dominant military power during the next 15 years. Further bolstering the strong position of the United States are its unparalleled economic power, its university system, and its investment in research and development—half of the total spent annually by the advanced industrial world. Many potential adversaries, as reflected in doctrinal writings and statements, see US military concepts, together with technology, as giving the United States the ability to expand its lead in conventional warfighting capabilities.

This perception among present and potential adversaries will continue to generate the pursuit of asymmetric capabilities against US forces and interests abroad as well as the territory of the United States. US opponents—state and such nonstate actors as drug lords, terrorists, and foreign insurgents—will not want to engage the US military on its terms. They will choose instead political and military strategies designed to dissuade the United States from using force, or, if the United States does use force, to exhaust American will, circumvent or minimize US strengths, and exploit perceived US weaknesses. Asymmetric challenges can arise across the spectrum of conflict that will confront US forces in a theater of operations or on US soil.

Central Asia: Regional Hot Spot?

The interests of Russia, China, and India—as well as of Iran and Turkey—will intersect in Central Asia; the states of that region will attempt to balance those powers as well as keep the United States and the West engaged to prevent their domination by an outside power. The greatest danger to the region, however, will not be a conflict between states, which is unlikely, but the corrosive impact of communal conflicts and political insurgencies, possibly abetted by outside actors and financed at least in part by narcotraffickers.

It is also generally recognized that the United States and other developed countries will continue to possess the political, economic, military, and technological advantages—including through National Missile and Theater Missile Defense systems—to reduce the gains of adversaries from lateral or "side-wise" technological improvements to their capabilities.

Threats to Critical Infrastructure. Some potential adversaries will seek ways to threaten the US homeland. The US national infrastructure—communications, transportation, financial transactions, energy networks—is vulnerable to disruption by physical and electronic attack because of its interdependent nature and by cyber attacks because of their dependence on computer networks. Foreign governments and groups will seek to exploit such vulnerabilities using conventional munitions, information operations, and even WMD. Over time, such attacks increasingly are likely to be delivered by computer networks rather than by conventional munitions, as the affinity for cyber attacks and the skill of US adversaries in employing them evolve. Cyber attacks will provide both state and nonstate adversaries new options for action against the United States beyond mere words but short of physical attack—strategic options that include selection of either nonlethal or lethal damage and the prospect of anonymity.

Information Operations. In addition to threatening the US national infrastructure, adversaries will seek to attack US military capabilities through electronic warfare, psychological operations, denial and deception, and the use of new technologies such as directed energy weapons or electromagnetic pulse weapons. The primary purpose would be to deny US forces information superiority, to prevent US weapons from working, and to undermine US domestic support for US actions. Adversaries also are likely to use cyber attacks to complicate US power projection in an era of decreasing permanent US military presence abroad by seeking to disrupt military networks during deployment operations—when they are most stressed. Many countries have programs to develop such technologies; few have the foresight or capability to fully integrate these various tools into a comprehensive attack. But they could develop such capabilities over the next decade and beyond.

Terrorism. Much of the terrorism noted earlier will be directed at the United States and its overseas interests. Most anti-US terrorism will be based on perceived ethnic, religious or cultural grievances. Terrorist groups will continue to find ways to attack US military and diplomatic facilities abroad. Such attacks are likely to expand increasingly to include US companies and American citizens. Middle East and Southwest Asian-based terrorists are the most likely to threaten the United States.

Weapons of Mass Destruction. WMD programs reflect the motivations and intentions of the governments that produce them and, therefore, can be altered by the change of a regime or by a regime's change of view. Linear projections of WMD are intended to assess what the picture will look like if changes in motivations and intentions do not occur.

Short- and medium-range ballistic missiles, particularly if armed with WMD, already pose a significant threat overseas to US interests, military forces, and allies. By 2015, the United States, barring major political changes in these countries, will face ICBM threats from North Korea, probably from Iran, and possibly from Iraq, in addition to long-standing threats from Russia and China.

- Weapons development programs, in many cases fueled by foreign assistance, have led to new capabilities—as illustrated by Iran's Shahab-3 launches in 1998 and 2000 and North Korea's Taepo Dong-1 space launch attempt in August 1998. In addition, some countries that have been traditional recipients of missile technologies have become exporters.

- Sales of ICBMs or space launch vehicles, which have inherent ICBM capabilities, could further increase the number of countries that will be able to threaten the United States with a missile strike.

The probability that a *missile armed with WMD* would be used against US forces or interests is higher today than during most of the Cold War and will continue to grow. The emerging missile threats will be mounted by countries possessing considerably fewer missiles with far less accuracy, yield, survivability, reliability, and range-payload capability than the strategic forces of the Soviet Union. North Korea's space launch attempt in 1998 demonstrated that P'yongyang is seeking a long-range missile capability that could be used against US forces and interests abroad and against US territory itself. Moreover, many of the countries developing longer-range missiles assess that the mere *threat* of their use would complicate US crisis decisionmaking and potentially would deter Washington from pursuing certain objectives.

Other means to deliver WMD against the United States will emerge, some cheaper and more reliable and accurate than early-generation ICBMs. The likelihood of an attack by these means is greater than that of a WMD attack with an ICBM. The goal of the adversary would be to move the weapon within striking distance by using short- and medium-range missiles deployed on surface ships or covert missions using military special operations forces or state intelligence services. Non-missile delivery means, however, do not provide the same prestige, deterrence, and coercive diplomacy associated with ICBMs.

Chemical and biological threats to the United States will become more widespread; such capabilities are easier to develop, hide, and deploy than nuclear weapons. Some terrorists or insurgents will attempt to use such weapons against US interests—against the United States itself, its forces or facilities overseas, or its allies. Moreover, the United States would be

---

WMD Proliferation and the Potential for Unconventional Warfare and Escalation

The risks of escalation inherent in direct armed conflict will be magnified by the availability of WMD; consequently, proliferation will tend to spur a reversion to prolonged, lower-level conflict by other means: intimidation, subversion, terrorism, proxies, and guerrilla operations. This trend already is evident between Israel and some of its neighbors and between India and Pakistan. In the event of war, urban fighting will be typical and consequently, civilian casualties will be high relative to those among combatants. Technology will count for less, and large, youthful, and motivated populations for more. Exploitation of communal divisions within an adversary's civil populations will be seen as a key to winning such conflicts—increasing their bitterness and thereby prolonging them.

---

affected by the use of such weapons anywhere in the world because Washington would be called on to help contain the damage and to provide scientific expertise and economic assistance to deal with the effects. Such weapons could be delivered through a variety of means, including missiles, unmanned aerial vehicles, or covertly via land, air, and sea.

Theater-range ballistic and cruise missile proliferation will continue. Most proliferation will involve systems a generation or two behind state of the art, but they will be substantially new capabilities for the states that acquire

Trends in Global Defense Spending and Armaments

Defense-related technologies will advance rapidly over the next 15 years—particularly precision weapons, information systems and communications. The development and integrated application of these technologies will occur mostly in the advanced countries, particularly the United States. Given the high costs and complexity of technical and operational integration, few nations will assign high priority to the indigenous development of such military technology.

- *Non-US global defense spending has dropped some 50 percent since the late 1980s. "Military modernization accounts," particularly procurement, have been hit hard.*

- *The global arms market has decreased by more than 50 percent during the same period.*

- *Indications are that global defense spending may be recovering from mid-1990s lows; part of East Asia, for example, could experience rises in defense spending over the next decade, but, overall, long-term spending patterns are uncertain.*

Over the past decade, a slow but persistent transformation has occurred in the arms procurement strategies of states. Many states are attempting to diversify sources of arms for reasons that vary from fears of arms embargoes, to declining defense budgets, or to a desire to acquire limited numbers of cutting-edge technologies. Their efforts include developing a mix of indigenous production; codeveloping, coproducing, or licensing production; purchasing entire weapon systems; or leasing capabilities. At the same time, many arms-producing states, confronted with declining domestic arms needs but determined to maintain defense industries, are commercializing defense production and aggressively expanding arms exports.

Together, the above factors suggest:

***Technology diffusion to those few states with a motivation to arm and the economic resources to do so will accelerate** as weapons and militarily relevant technologies are moved rapidly and routinely across national borders in response to increasingly commercial rather than security calculations. For such militarily related technologies as the Global Positioning System, satellite imagery, and communications, **technological superiority will be difficult to maintain for very long**. In an environment of broad technological diffusion, nonmaterial elements of military power—strategy, doctrine, and training—will increase in importance over the next 15 years in deciding combat outcomes.*

(continued)

59

them. Such missiles will be capable of delivering WMD or conventional payloads inter-regionally against fixed targets. Major air and sea ports, logistics bases and facilities, troop concentrations, and fixed communications nodes increasingly will be at risk.

- Land-attack cruise missiles probably will be more accurate than ballistic missiles.

Access to Space. US competitors and adversaries realize the degree to which access to space is critical to US military power, and by 2015 they will have made strides in countering US space dominance. International commercialization of space will give states and nonstate adversaries access rivaling today's major space powers in such areas as high-resolution reconnaissance and weather prediction, global encrypted communications, and precise navigation. When combined, such services will provide adversaries who are aware of US and allied force deployments the capability for precise targeting and global coordination of operations. Moreover, many adversaries will have developed capabilities to degrade US space assets—in particular, with attacks against ground facilities, electronic warfare, and denial and deception. By 2015, several countries will have such counterspace technologies as improved space-object tracking, signal jamming, and directed-energy weapons such as low-power lasers.

Major Regions

The following snapshots of individual regions result from our assessment of trends and from estimates by regional experts as to where specific nations will be in 15 years. To make these judgments, we have distilled the views

60

expressed by many outside experts in our conferences and workshops. The results are intended to stimulate debate, not to endorse one view over another.

East and Southeast Asia
Regional Trends. East Asia over the next 15 years will be characterized by uneven economic dynamism—both between and within states—political and national assertiveness rather than ideology, and potential for strategic tension if not outright conflict.

The states of the region will be led by generally nationalistic governments eschewing ideology and focusing on nation-building and development. These states will broadly accommodate international norms on the free flow of information to modernize their economies, open markets, and fight international crime and disease. They also will encounter pressure for greater political pluralism, democracy, and respect for human rights. Failure to meet popular expectations probably will result in leaders being voted

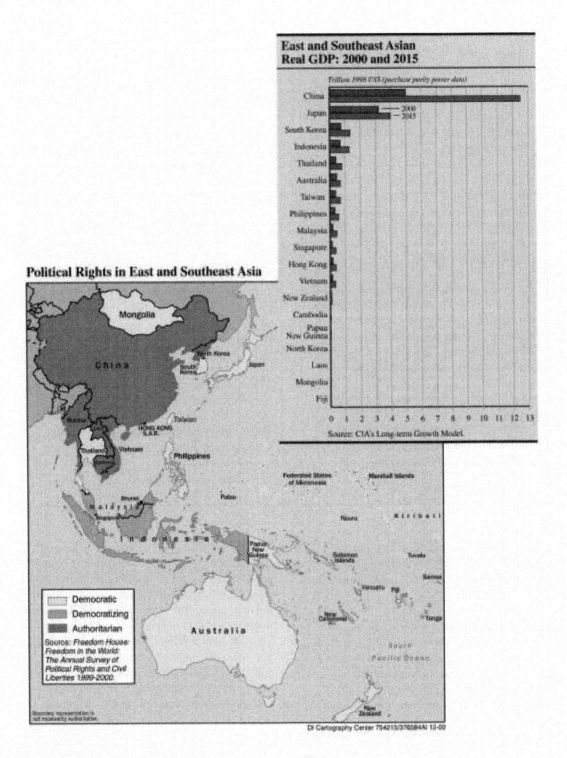

East and Southeast Asian Real GDP: 2000 and 2015

Trillion 1998 US$ (purchase parity power data)

Legend:
- 2000
- 2015

Countries (top to bottom): China, Japan, South Korea, Indonesia, Thailand, Australia, Taiwan, Philippines, Malaysia, Singapore, Hong Kong, Vietnam, New Zealand, Cambodia, Papua New Guinea, North Korea, Laos, Mongolia, Fiji

X-axis: 0 1 2 3 4 5 6 7 8 9 10 11 12 13

Source: CIA's Long-term Growth Model.

Political Rights in East and Southeast Asia

Legend:
- Democratic
- Democratizing
- Authoritarian

Source: Freedom House: Freedom in the World: The Annual Survey of Political Rights and Civil Liberties 1999-2000.

Boundary representation is not necessarily authoritative.

DI Cartography Center 754215/376584AI 12-00

out of office in democratic states or in widespread demonstrations and violence leading to regime collapse in authoritarian states.

Political and Security Trends. The major power realignments and the more fluid post-Cold War security environment in the region will raise serious questions about how regional leaders will handle nascent great-power rivalries (the US-China, China-Japan, China-India), related regional "hot spots" (Taiwan, Korea, South China Sea), the future of challenged political regimes (Indonesia, North Korea absent unification, China), and communal tensions and minority issues (in China, Indonesia, the Philippines, and Malaysia). On balance, the number and range of rivalries and potential flashpoints suggest a better-than-even chance that episodes of military confrontation and conflict will erupt over the next 15 years.

The implications of the rise of China as an economic and increasingly capable regional military power—even as the influence of Communism and authoritarianism weakens—pose the greatest uncertainty in the area. Adding to uncertainty are the prospects for—and implications of—Korean unification over the next 15 years, and the evolution of Japan's regional leadership aspirations and capabilities.

Instability in Russia and Central Asia, and the nuclear standoff between India and Pakistan will be peripheral but still important in East Asian security calculations. The Middle East will become increasingly important as a primary source of energy.

Economic Dynamism. While governments in the region generally will accept the need to accommodate international norms on ownership, markets, trade, and investment, they will

seek to block or slow the perceived adverse economic, political, and social consequences of globalization.

The most likely economic outlook will be that rich societies—Japan, Korea, Hong Kong, Taiwan, Singapore, and pockets in China and elsewhere—will get richer, with Japan likely to continue to be a leader in S&T development and applications for commercial use. In contrast, the poor societies—Vietnam, Cambodia, Laos, and rural areas in western China and elsewhere—will fall further behind. Greater economic links are likely to have been forged between Taiwan, Hong Kong, and South China as a result of the development of investment and infrastructure. China will be increasingly integrated into the world economy through foreign direct investment, trade, and international capital markets. Energy markets will have drawn the region more closely together despite lingering issues of ownership of resources and territorial disputes.

Key uncertainties will persist on economic performance and political stability, including the rising costs of pensions and services for Japan's aging population; the adequacy of energy and water for China, political leadership in Indonesia and China, and the impact of AIDS in Cambodia, Thailand, and Vietnam.

Regional Interaction. Given the weakness of regional political-security arrangements, the US political, economic, and security presence will remain pronounced. At the same time, many countries in the region will remain uncertain about US objectives, apprehensive of both US withdrawal and US unilateralism. Key states, most significantly China and Japan, will continue "hedging," by using diplomacy, military preparations and other means to ensure that their particular interests will be safeguarded, especially in case the regional situation deteriorates.

Japan and others will seek to maintain a US presence, in part to counter China's influence. Economic and other ties will bind Japan and China, but historical, territorial, and strategic differences will underline continuing wariness between the two. China will want good economic ties to the United States but also will nurture links to Russia and others to counter the possibility of US pressure against it and to weaken US support for Taiwan and the US security posture in East Asia. US-China confrontations over Taiwan or over broader competing security interests are possible.

Although preserving the US alliance, Japanese leaders also will be less certain they can rely on the United States to deal with some security contingencies. More confident of their ability to handle security issues independently, they will pursue initiatives internally and overseas that are designed to safeguard Japanese interests without direct reference to the US alliance.

South Asia
Regional Trends. The widening strategic and economic gaps between the two principal powers, India and Pakistan—and the dynamic interplay between their mutual hostility and the instability in Central Asia—will define the South Asia region in 2015.

- India will be the unrivaled regional power with a large military—including naval and nuclear capabilities—and a dynamic and growing economy. The widening India-Pakistan gap—destabilizing in its own right—will be accompanied by deep political, economic, and social disparities within both states.

- Pakistan will be more fractious, isolated, and dependent on international financial assistance.

- Other South Asian states—Bangladesh, Sri Lanka, and Nepal—will be drawn closer to and more dependent on India and its economy. Afghanistan will likely remain weak and a destabilizing force in the region and the world.

Wary of China, India will look increasingly to the West, but its need for oil and desire to balance Arab ties to Pakistan will lead to strengthened ties to Persian Gulf states as well.

Demographic Challenges. Although population growth rates in South Asia will decline, population still will grow by nearly 30 percent by 2015. India's population alone will grow to more than 1.2 billion. Pakistan's projected growth from 140 million to about 195 million in 2015 will put a major strain on an economy already unable to meet the basic needs of the current population. The percentage of urban dwellers will climb steadily from the current 25-30 percent of the population to between 40-50 percent, leading to continued deterioration in the overall quality of urban life. Differential population growth patterns will exacerbate inequalities in wealth. Ties between provincial and central governments throughout the region will be strained.

Resource and Environmental Challenges. Water will remain South Asia's most vital and most contested natural resource. Continued population and economic growth and expansion of irrigated agriculture over the next 15 years will increasingly stress water resources, and pollution of surface and groundwater will be a serious challenge. In India, per capita

Jammu and Kashmir: Ethnic Mix of a Disputed State

Legend:
- Buddhist
- Hindu
- Muslim

China

Pakistan

Skardu

Kashmir

Line of Control

Kel

Keran

Kupwara

Kargil

Muzaffarabad

Lipa Valley

Kishtil

Baramula

Jammu and Kashmir State

Leh

Srinagar

Vale of Kashmir

Murree

Rawala Kot

ISLAMABAD

Punch

Rawalpindi

India

Kotli

Rajauri

Jhelum

Akhnur

Udhampur

Jammu

Nagrota

Gujranwala

Sialkot

Pakistan

Source: Kashmir Study Group: Kashmir: A Way Forward, February 2000

Lahore

Amritsar

DI Cartography Center 753976AI 12-00

Area of main map

Pakistan

India

Indian Ocean

water availability is likely to drop by 50-75 percent. Because many of the region's waterways are interstate, water could become a source of renewed friction. Deforestation in India and Nepal will exacerbate pollution, flooding, and land degradation in Bangladesh.

India in 2015. Indian democracy will remain strong, albeit more factionalized by the secular-Hindu nationalist debate, growing differentials among regions and the increase in competitive party politics. India's economy, long repressed by the heavy hand of regulation, is likely to achieve sustained growth to the degree reforms are implemented. High-technology companies will be the most dynamic agents and will lead the thriving service sector in four key urban centers—Mumbai, New Delhi, Bangalore, and Chennai. Computer software services and customized applications will continue to expand as India strengthens economic ties to key international markets. Industries such as pharmaceuticals and agro-processing also will compete globally. Numerous factors provide India a competitive advantage in the global economy. It has the largest English-speaking population in the developing world; its education system produces millions of scientific and technical personnel. India has a growing business-minded middle class eager to strengthen ties to the outside world, and the large Indian expatriate population provides strong links to key markets around the world.

Despite rapid economic growth, more than half a billion Indians will remain in dire poverty. Harnessing technology to improve agriculture will be India's main challenge in alleviating poverty in 2015. The widening gulf between "have" and "have-not" regions and disagreements over the pace and nature of reforms will be a source of domestic strife. Rapidly growing, poorer northern states will continue to drain resources in subsidies and social welfare benefits.

Pakistan in 2015. Pakistan, our conferees concluded, will not recover easily from decades of political and economic mismanagement, divisive politics, lawlessness, corruption and ethnic friction. Nascent democratic reforms will produce little change in the face of opposition from an entrenched political elite and radical Islamic parties. Further domestic decline would benefit Islamic political activists, who may significantly increase their role in national politics and alter the makeup and cohesion of the military—once Pakistan's most capable institution. In a climate of continuing domestic turmoil, the central government's control probably will be reduced to the Punjabi heartland and the economic hub of Karachi.

Other Regional States. Prospects for Afghanistan, Bangladesh, and Sri Lanka in 2015 appear bleak. Decades of foreign domination and civil war have devastated Afghanistan's society and economy, and the country is likely to remain internationally isolated, a major narcotics exporter, and a haven for Islamic radicals and terrorist groups. Bangladesh will not abandon democracy but will be characterized by coalitions or weak one-party governments, fragile institutions of governance, deep-seated leadership squabbles, and no notion of a loyal opposition.

Security and Political Concerns Predominate. The threat of major conflict between India and Pakistan will overshadow all other regional issues during the next 15 years. Continued turmoil in Afghanistan and Pakistan will spill over into Kashmir and other areas of the subcontinent, prompting Indian leaders to take more aggressive preemptive and retaliatory actions. India's conventional military advantage over Pakistan will widen as a result of New Delhi's superior economic position. India will also continue to build up its ocean-going navy to dominate the Indian Ocean transit routes used for delivery of Persian Gulf oil to Asia. The decisive shift in conventional military power in India's favor over the coming years potentially will make the region more volatile and unstable. Both India and Pakistan will see weapons

Projected Demographic Trends in Eurasia

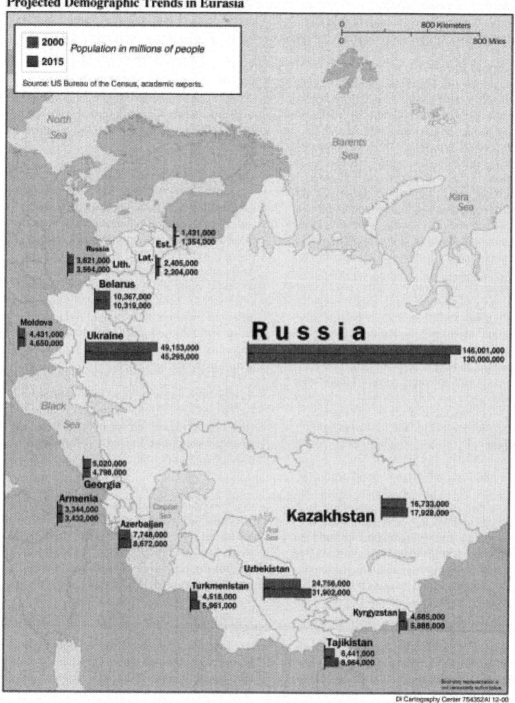

Population in millions of people

2000
2015

Source: US Bureau of the Census, academic experts.

0 — 800 Kilometers
0 — 800 Miles

Est. 1,431,000 / 1,354,000
Russia 3,621,000 / 3,564,000 — Lith. — Lat. 2,405,000 / 2,204,000
Belarus 10,367,000 / 10,319,000
Moldova 4,431,000 / 4,650,000
Ukraine 49,153,000 / 45,295,000
Russia 146,001,000 / 130,000,000
Georgia 5,020,000 / 4,796,000
Armenia 3,344,000 / 3,432,000
Azerbaijan 7,748,000 / 8,672,000
Kazakhstan 16,733,000 / 17,928,000
Uzbekistan 24,756,000 / 31,902,000
Turkmenistan 4,518,000 / 5,961,000
Kyrgyzstan 4,685,000 / 5,886,000
Tajikistan 6,441,000 / 8,964,000

DI Cartography Center 754302AI 12-00

67

of mass destruction as a strategic imperative and will continue to amass nuclear warheads and build a variety of missile delivery systems.

Russia and Eurasia

Regional Trends. Uncertainties abound about the future internal configuration, geopolitical dynamics, and degree of turbulence within and among former Soviet states. Russia and the other states of Eurasia are likely to fall short in resolving critical impediments to economic and political reform in their struggle to manage the negative legacies of the Soviet period. Changing demographics, chronic economic difficulties, and continued questions about governance will constrain Russia's ability to project its power beyond the former Soviet republics to the south, complicate Ukraine's efforts to draw closer to the West, and retard the development of stable, open political structures throughout the Caucasus and Central Asia. Those states that could make progress on the basis of potential energy revenues are likely to fail because of corruption and the absence of structural economic reform. The rapid pace of scientific and technological innovation, as well as globalization, will leave these states further behind the West as well as behind the major emerging markets.

The economic challenges to these countries will remain daunting: insufficient structural reform, poor productivity in agriculture as compared with Western standards, decaying infrastructure and environmental degradation. Corruption and organized crime, sustained by drug trafficking, money laundering, and other illegal enterprises and, in several instances, protected by corrupt political allies, will persist.

Demographic pressures also will affect the economic performance and political cohesiveness of these states. Because of low birthrates and falling life expectancy among males, the populations of the Slavic core and much of the Caucasus will continue to decline; Russian experts predict that the country's population could fall from 146 million at present to 130-135 million by 2015. At the other end of the spectrum, the Central Asian countries will face a growing youth cohort that will peak around 2010 before resuming a more gradual pattern of population growth.

The centrality of Russia will continue to diminish, and by 2015 "Eurasia" will be a geographic term lacking a unifying political, economic, and cultural reality. Russia and the western Eurasian States will continue to orient themselves toward Europe but will remain essentially outside of it. Because of geographic proximity and cultural affinities, the Caucasus will be closer politically to their neighbors to the south and west, with Central Asia drawing closer to South Asia and China. Nonetheless, important interdependencies will remain, primarily in the energy sphere.

Russia will remain the most important actor in the former Soviet Union. Its power relative to others in the region and neighboring areas will have declined, however, and it will continue to lack the resources to impose its will.

The Soviet economic inheritance will continue to plague Russia. Besides a crumbling physical infrastructure, years of environmental neglect are taking a toll on the population, a toll made worse by such societal costs of transition as alcoholism, cardiac diseases, drugs, and a worsening health delivery system. Russia's population is not only getting smaller, but it is becoming less and less healthy and thus less able to serve as an engine of economic recovery. In macro economic terms Russia's GDP probably has bottomed out. Russia, nevertheless, is still likely to fall short in its efforts to become fully integrated into the global financial and trading system by 2015. Even under a best case scenario of five percent annual economic growth, Russia would attain an economy less than one-fifth the size of that of the United States.

Many Russian futures are possible, ranging from political resurgence to dissolution. The general drift, however, is toward authoritarianism, although not to the extreme extent of the Soviet period. The factors favoring this course are President Putin's own bent toward hierarchical rule from Moscow; the population's general support of this course as an antidote to the messiness and societal disruption of the post-Soviet transition; the ability of the ruling elite to hold on to power because of the lack of effective national opposition, thus making that elite accountable only to itself; and the ongoing shift of tax resources from the regions to the center. This centralizing tendency will contribute to dysfunctional governance. Effective governance is nearly impossible under such centralization for a country as large and diverse as Russia and lacking well-ordered, disciplined national bureaucracies. Recentralization, however, will be constrained by the interconnectedness brought about by the global information revolution, and by the gradual, although uneven, growth of civil society.

Russia will focus its foreign policy goals on reestablishing lost influence in the former Soviet republics to the south, fostering ties to Europe and Asia, and presenting itself as a significant player vis-a-vis the United States. Its energy resources will be an important lever for these endeavors. However, its domestic ills will frustrate its efforts to reclaim its great power status. Russia will maintain the second largest nuclear arsenal in the world as the last vestige of its old status. The net outcome of these trends will be a Russia that remains internally weak and institutionally linked to the international system primarily through its permanent seat on the UN Security Council.

Ukraine's path to the West will be constrained by widespread corruption, the power of criminal organizations, and lingering questions over its commitment to the rule of law. Kiev will remain vulnerable to Russian pressures, primarily because of its continued energy dependence, but Ukrainians of all political stripes and likely to opt for independence rather than reintegration into Russia's sphere of influence.

In 2015, the *South Caucasus* will remain in flux because of unresolved local conflicts, weak economic fundamentals, and continued Russian meddling. *Georgia* probably will have achieved a measure of political and economic stability, fueled in part by energy transit revenues, but it will remain the focus of Russian attention in the region. *Armenia* will remain largely isolated and is likely to remain a Russian—or possibly Iranian—client and, therefore, a regional wild card. *Azerbaijan's* success in developing its energy sector is unlikely to bring widespread prosperity: Baku will be a one-sector economy with pervasive corruption at all levels of society.

In *Central Asia*, social, environmental, religious, and possibly ethnic strains will grow. Wasteful water-intensive practices and pollution of ground water and arable land will lead to continued shortages for agricultural and energy generation. The high birthrates of the 1980s and early 1990s will lead to strains on education, healthcare, and social services. The region also is likely to be the scene of increased competition among surrounding powers—Russia, China, India, Iran, and possibly Turkey—for control, influence, and access to energy resources. Developments in Afghanistan and Pakistan will threaten regional stability.

Growth in Population From 2000 to 2015

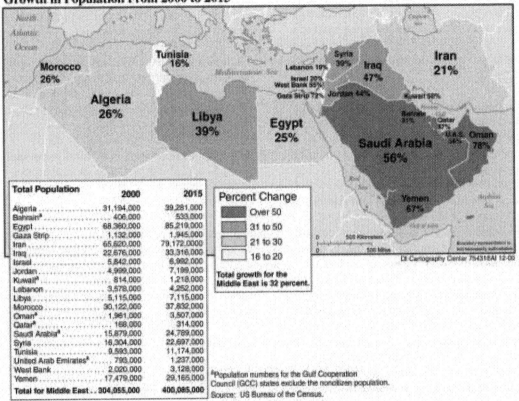

Total Population	2000	2015
Algeria	31,194,000	39,281,000
Bahrain[a]	406,000	533,000
Egypt	68,360,000	85,219,000
Gaza Strip	1,132,000	1,945,000
Iran	65,620,000	79,172,0000
Iraq	22,676,000	33,316,000
Israel	5,842,000	6,992,000
Jordan	4,999,000	7,189,000
Kuwait[a]	814,000	1,218,000
Lebanon	3,578,000	4,252,000
Libya	5,115,000	7,115,000
Morocco	30,122,000	37,832,000
Oman[a]	1,961,000	3,507,000
Qatar[a]	168,000	314,000
Saudi Arabia[a]	15,879,000	24,789,000
Syria	16,304,000	22,697,000
Tunisia	9,593,000	11,174,000
United Arab Emirates[a]	793,000	1,237,000
West Bank	2,020,000	3,128,000
Yemen	17,479,000	29,165,000
Total for Middle East	**304,055,000**	**400,085,000**

Percent Change
- Over 50
- 31 to 50
- 21 to 30
- 16 to 20

Total growth for the Middle East is 32 percent.

[a]Population numbers for the Gulf Cooperation Council (GCC) states exclude the noncitizen population.
Source: US Bureau of the Census.

DI Cartography Center 754316AI 12-00

The Middle East and North Africa

Regimes in the region—from Morocco to Iran—will have to cope with demographic, economic and societal pressures from within and globalization from without. No single ideology or philosophy will unite any one state or group of states in response to these challenges, although popular resentment of globalization as a Western intrusion will be widespread. Political Islam in various forms will be an attractive alternative for millions of Muslims throughout the region, and some radical variants will continue to be divisive social and political forces.

By 2015, Israel will have attained a cold peace with its neighbors, with only limited social, economic, and cultural ties. There will be a Palestinian state, but Israeli-Palestinian tensions will persist and occasionally erupt into crises. Old rivalries among core states—Egypt, Syria, Iraq, and Iran—will reemerge. International attention will shift anew to the Persian Gulf, an increasingly important source of energy resources to fuel the global economy, and oil revenues anticipated for Iraq, Iran, and Saudi Arabia in particular will provide strategic—and potentially destabilizing—options for those states. New relationships between geographic regions could emerge between North Africa and Europe (on trade); India, China and the Persian Gulf (on energy); and Israel, Turkey, and India (on economic, technical, and in the case of Turkey, security considerations).

A key driver for the Middle East over the next 15 years will be demographic pressures, specifically how to provide jobs, housing, public services, and subsidies for rapidly growing and increasingly urban populations. By 2015, in much of the Middle East populations will be significantly larger, poorer, more urban, and more disillusioned. In nearly all Middle Eastern countries, more than half the population is now under 20 years of age. These populations will continue to have very large youth cohorts through 2015, with the labor force growing at an average rate of 3.1 percent per year. The problem of job placement is compounded by weak educational systems producing a generation lacking the technical and problem-solving skills required for economic growth.

Globalization. With the exception of Israel, Middle Eastern states will view globalization more as a challenge than an opportunity. Although the Internet will remain confined to a small elite due to relatively high cost, undeveloped infrastructures, and cultural obstacles, the information revolution and other technological advances probably will have a net destabilizing effect on the Middle East by raising expectations, increasing income disparities, and eroding the power of regimes to control information or mold popular opinion. Attracting foreign direct investment will also be difficult: except for the energy sector, investors will tend to shy away from these countries, discouraged by overbearing state sectors; heavy, opaque, and

arbitrary government regulation; underdeveloped financial sectors; inadequate physical infrastructure; and the threat of political instability.

Political Change. Most Middle Eastern governments recognize the need for economic restructuring and even a modicum of greater political participation, but they will proceed cautiously, fearful of undermining their rule. As some governments or sectors embrace the new economy and civil society while others cling to more traditional paradigms, inequities between and within states will grow. Islamists could come to power in states that are beginning to become pluralist and in which entrenched secular elites have lost their appeal.

Sub-Saharan Africa
Regional Trends. The interplay of demographics and disease—as well as poor governance—will be the major determinants of Africa's increasing international marginalization in 2015. Most African states will miss out on the economic growth engendered elsewhere by globalization and by scientific and technological advances. Only a few countries will do better, while a handful of states will have hardly any relevance to the lives of their citizens. As Sub-Saharan Africa's multiple and interconnected problems are compounded, ethnic and communal tensions will intensify, periodically escalating into open conflict, often spreading across borders and sometimes spawning secessionist states.

In the absence of a major medical breakthrough, the relentless progression of AIDS and other diseases will decimate the economically productive adult population, sharply accentuate the continent's youth bulge, and generate a

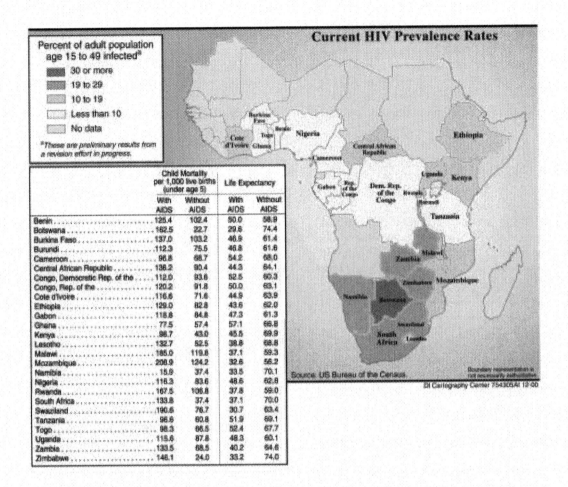

Current HIV Prevalence Rates

Percent of adult population age 15 to 49 infected*

- 30 or more
- 19 to 29
- 10 to 19
- Less than 10
- No data

*These are preliminary results from a revision effort in progress.

Source: US Bureau of the Census.

DI Cartography Center 754305AI 12-00

	Child Mortality per 1,000 live births (under age 5)		Life Expectancy	
	With AIDS	Without AIDS	With AIDS	Without AIDS
Benin	125.4	102.4	50.0	58.9
Botswana	162.5	22.7	29.6	74.4
Burkina Faso	137.0	103.2	46.9	61.4
Burundi	112.3	75.5	46.8	61.6
Cameroon	96.8	68.7	54.2	68.0
Central African Republic	136.2	90.4	44.3	64.1
Congo, Democratic Rep. of the	112.0	93.6	52.5	60.3
Congo, Rep. of the	120.2	91.8	50.0	63.1
Cote d'Ivoire	116.6	71.6	44.9	63.9
Ethiopia	129.0	82.8	43.6	62.0
Gabon	118.8	84.8	47.3	61.3
Ghana	77.5	57.4	57.1	66.8
Kenya	96.7	43.0	45.5	69.9
Lesotho	132.7	52.5	38.8	68.8
Malawi	185.0	119.8	37.1	59.3
Mozambique	208.9	124.2	32.6	55.2
Namibia	18.9	37.4	33.5	70.1
Nigeria	118.3	83.6	48.6	62.8
Rwanda	167.5	105.8	37.8	59.0
South Africa	133.8	37.4	37.1	70.0
Swaziland	190.6	76.7	30.7	63.4
Tanzania	96.6	60.8	51.9	69.1
Togo	98.3	66.5	52.4	67.7
Uganda	115.6	87.8	48.3	60.1
Zambia	133.5	68.5	40.2	64.6
Zimbabwe	146.1	24.0	33.2	74.0

huge cohort of orphaned children. This condition will strain the ability of the extended family system to cope and will contribute to higher levels of dissatisfaction, crime, and political volatility.

Poverty and poor governance will further deplete natural resources and drive rapid urbanization. As impoverished people flee unproductive rural areas, many cities will double in population by 2015, but resources will be inadequate to provide the needed expansion of water systems, sewers, and health facilities. Cities will be sources of crime and instability as ethnic and religious differences exacerbate the competition for ever scarcer jobs and resources. The number of malnourished people will increase by more than 20 percent and the potential for famine will persist where the combination of internal conflict and recurring natural disasters prevents or limits relief efforts.

Economic Prospects. Conditions for economic development in Sub-Saharan Africa are limited by the persistence of conflicts, poor political leadership and endemic corruption, and uncertain weather conditions. Africa's most talented individuals will shun the public sector or be lured abroad by greater income and security. Effective and conscientious leaders are unlikely to emerge from undemocratic and corrupt societies.

- Most technological advances in the next 15 years—with the possible exception of genetically modified crops—will not have substantial positive impact on the African economies.

- Although West Africa will play an increasing role in global energy markets, providing 25 percent of North American oil imports in 2015, the pattern of oil wealth fostering corruption rather than economic development will continue.

There will be exceptions to this bleak overall outlook. The quality of governance, rather than resource endowments, will be the key determinant of development and differentiation among African states.

South Africa and Nigeria, the continent's largest economies, will remain the dominant powers in the region through 2015. But their ability to function as economic locomotives and stabilizers in their regions will be constrained by large unmet domestic demands for resources to stimulate employment, growth, and social services, including dealing with AIDS. Even a robust South Africa will not exert a strong pull on its partners in the Southern African Development Community (SADC). The success of the South African economy will be more closely tied to its relationship with the larger global economy than with Sub-Saharan Africa.

Role of Nonstate Actors. The atrophy of special relationships between European powers and their former colonies in Africa will be virtually complete by 2015. Filling the void will

Ethnic, political, and religious conflicts in Sub-Saharan Africa have generated tens of thousands of civilian casualties killed or wounded and created massive refugee flows. In 1998, these children found shelter in a Rwandan refugee camp. Conflicts in Sub-Saharan Africa and the humanitarian crises they generate will continue to require the attention and assistance of the international community in the coming years.

DI Design Center 377051AI 12-00

be international organizations and nonstate actors of all types: transnational religious institutions; international nonprofit organizations, international crime syndicates and drug traffickers; foreign mercenaries; and international terrorists seeking safehavens.

- Fundamentalist movements, especially proselytizing Islamic groups, will plow fertile ground as Africans seek alternative ways to meet their basic needs.

- Internal conflicts will attract—and leaders will in some cases welcome —foreign criminal organizations or mercenaries to assist in the plundering of national assets, while faltering regimes will willingly trade their sovereignty for cash.

International organizations will be heavily engaged in Sub-Saharan Africa over the next 15 years, given its growing needs and slow

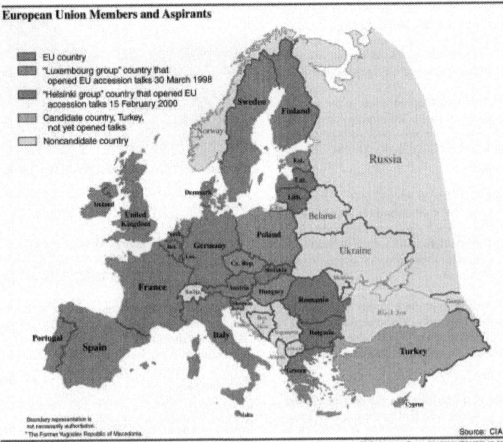

EU country

"Luxembourg group" country that
opened EU accession talks 30 March 1998

"Helsinki group" country that opened EU
accession talks 15 February 2000

Candidate country, Turkey,
not yet opened talks

Noncandidate country

Boundary representation is
not necessarily authoritative.
* The Former Yugoslav Republic of Macedonia.

Source: CIA

DI Cartography Center 754300AI (R00587) 12-00

growth relative to other regions. Africa will
continue to receive more development assistance per capita than other regions of the world.

• The international financial institutions will be
a continuing presence in Africa, as many
donor countries funnel development assistance through them.

• The perpetuation of poor governance and
communal conflicts in a region awash with
guns will generate frequent natural and man-
made humanitarian crises, precipitating international humanitarian relief efforts.

• The Economic Community of West African
States (ECOWAS) and the SADC will be the
primary economic and political instruments
through which the continental powers, Nigeria and South Africa, exert their leadership.

Europe
Regional Trends. Most of Europe in 2015 will
be relatively peaceful and wealthy. Its residents
will do extensive business with the rest of the
world but politically will be more inward-look-
ing than the citizens of Europe in 2000. Look-

ing out to 2015, Europe's agenda will be to put in place the final components of EU integration; to take advantage of globalization; to sustain a strong IT and S&T base to tackle changing demographics; and to wean the Balkans away from virulent nationalism.

EU enlargement, institutional reform, and a common foreign, security and defense policy will play out over the next 15 years, so that by 2015 the final contours of the "European project" are likely to be firmly set. Having absorbed at least 10 new members, the European Union will have achieved its geographic and institutional limits.

- As a consequence of long delays in gaining EU entry (and the after-effects of actual membership), leaders in some Central/Eastern Europe countries will be susceptible to pressures from authoritarian, nationalist forces on both the left and right. These forces will capitalize on public resentment about the effects of EU policy and globalization, including unemployment, foreign ownership, and cultural penetration.

- The EU will not include Russia. The Europeans, nevertheless, will seek to engage Moscow—encouraging stability and maintaining dialogue. Although Russia will continue to recede in importance to the European governments, they will use US handling of Russia as a barometer of how well or poorly Washington is exerting leadership and defending European interests.

Economic Reform & Globalization. EU governments will continue to seek a "third way" between state control and unbridled capitalism: piecemeal and often unavowed economic reform driven in part by an ever denser network of overseas business relationships and changes in corporate governance. Lingering labor market rigidity and state regulation will hamper restructuring, retooling, and reinvestment strategies. Europe will trail the United States in entrepreneurship and innovation as governments seek ways to balance encouragement of these factors against social effects. Thus, Europe will not achieve fully the dreams of parity with the United States as a shaper of the global economic system.

In Prague, Vienna, and other European capitals, protestors have questioned the merits of globalization. By 2015, Europe will have globalized more extensively than some of its political rhetoric will suggest. It also will have less difficulty than other regions coping with rapid change because of high education and technological levels. States will continue to push private sector competitiveness in the international market. Three of the top five information technology centers in the world will be in Europe: London, Munich, and Paris.

Many Europeans will see the role of foreign policy as protecting their social and cultural identities from the "excesses" of globalization—and from its "superpatron," the United States. One of the ways in which leaders will respond will be to clamor for greater political control over international financial and trade institutions.

The aging of the population and low birthrates will be major challenges to European prosperity and cohesion. Greater percentages of state budgets will have to be allocated to the aging, while, at the same time, there will be significant, chronic shortages both of highly skilled workers in IT and other professions and unskilled workers in basic services. Legal and illegal immigration will mitigate labor shortages to a limited extent but at a cost in terms of social friction and crime. As EU governments grapple with immigration policy and European and national identity, anti-immigrant sentiment will figure more prominently in the political arena throughout Western Europe.

Turkey. The future direction of Turkey, both internally and geopolitically, will have a major impact on the region, and on US and Western interests. Shifting political dynamics; debates over identity, ethnicity and the role of religion in the state; and the further development of civil society will figure prominently in Turkey's domestic agenda. The road to Turkish membership in the EU will be long and difficult, and EU member states will evaluate Turkey's candidacy not only on the basis of economic performance, but on how well it tackles this comprehensive agenda. Part of Turkey's success will hinge on the effectiveness of a growing private sector in advancing Turkey's reform efforts and its goal of full integration in the West. NATO's involvement in the Ballkans and expected enlargement in southern Europe will increase ties between Turkey and the West.

By dint of its history, location, and interests, Turkey will continue to pay attention to its neighbors to the north—in the Caucasus and Central Asia—and to the south and east—Syria, Iraq and Iran. With few exceptions, these states will continue to struggle with questions of governance. As Turkey crafts policies toward the countries in these regions, no single issue will dominate its national security agenda. Rather, Ankara will find itself having to cope with regional rivalries—including what policies to adopt toward internal and interstate conflicts—proliferation of weapons of mass destruction, the politics and economics of energy transport, and water rights.

Europe and the World. Europe's agenda will require it to demonstrate influence in world affairs commensurate with its size in population and economic strength. The EU's global reach will be based primarily on economics: robust trade and investment links to the United States and growing ties to East and Southeast Asia and Latin America.

In dealing with matters outside the region, European leaders will construe their global responsibilities as building legal mechanisms, encouraging diplomatic contact, and—to a lesser extent—providing nonmilitary aid. They will respond sporadically to foreign crises—either through the UN or in ad hoc "coalitions of the willing" with Washington or others—but they will not make strong and consistent overseas commitments, particularly in regard to sending troops.

Transatlantic Links. Economic issues will have overtaken security issues in importance by 2015, and the United States will see its relations with Europe defined increasingly through the EU, not only on the basis of trade but in the context of using economic tools—such as aid and preferential trading regimes—to underwrite peace initiatives.

By 2015, NATO will have accepted many, but not all, Central/Eastern European countries. European Security and Defense Policy will be set in terms of partnership with, rather than replacement of, NATO.

Canada
Trends. Canada will be a full participant in the globalization process in 2015 and a leading player in the Americas after the United States, along with Mexico and Brazil. Ottawa will still

Average Annual Population Growth From 1998 to 2015

Average Annual Population Growth Rate, 1998 to 2015	Percent		
	Age 0-14	Age 15-64	Age 65+
Argentina	0.0	1.3	1.6
Bolivia	0.5	2.6	2.8
Brazil	0.0	1.4	2.8
Chile	-0.5	1.4	3.1
Colombia	-0.2	2.0	2.8
Costa Rica	-0.7	1.9	3.9
Cuba	-1.6	0.4	2.7
Dominican Republic	-0.4	2.0	3.2
Ecuador	-0.3	2.2	2.9
El Salvador	0.3	2.3	2.1
Guatemala	0.7	3.1	2.1
Haiti	0.3	2.4	1.7
Honduras	0.5	3.1	2.8
Jamaica	-0.8	1.5	1.6
Mexico	-0.2	1.9	3.1
Nicaragua	0.5	3.2	3.1
Panama	-0.5	1.8	3.1
Paraguay	0.2	2.8	3.0
Peru	0.1	2.0	2.8
Trinidad and Tobago	-0.9	1.1	2.6
Uruguay	-0.2	0.8	0.7
Venezuela	-0.2	2.2	3.8
Latin America & Caribbean	-0.1	1.8	2.7

Source: World Bank.

DI Cartography Center 753975AI (R01418) 12-00

be grappling with the political, demographic, and cultural impact of heavy Asian immigration in the West as well as residual nationalist sentiment in French-speaking Quebec. The vast and diverse country, however, will remain stable amidst constant, dynamic change.

Ottawa will continue to emphasize the importance of education, and especially science and technology, for the new economy. Canada also will promote policies designed to stem the flow of skilled workers south and will seek to attract skilled immigrants—especially professionals from East and South Asia—to ensure that Canada will be able to take full advantage of global opportunities. The question of Quebec's place in the country will continue to stir national debate.

Canada's status as the pre-eminent US economic partner will be even more pronounced in 2015. National sensitivity to encroaching US culture will remain, even as the two economies become more integrated. Ottawa will retain its interests in the stability and prosperity of East Asia because of growing Canadian economic, cultural, and demographic links to the Pacific region. As additional trade links with Latin America are developed through the North American Free Trade Agreement and a likely Free Trade Area of the Americas, Canada increasingly will take advantage of developments in the Western hemisphere. Although Canadians will focus more on Latin America and less on Europe, they will still look to NATO as the cornerstone of Western security. Like Europeans, Canadians will judge US global leadership in terms of the relationship with Russia, especially regarding strategic arms and National Missile Defense (NMD).

Despite the relatively small size of Canada's armed forces, Ottawa still will seek to participate in global and regional discussions on the future of international peacekeeping. Canada will continue to build on its traditional support for international organizations by working to ensure a more effective UN and greater respect for international treaties, norms, and regimes. Canadians will be sympathetic to calls for greater political "management" of globalization to help mitigate adverse impacts on the environment and ensure that globalization's benefits reach less advantaged regions and states.

Latin America
Regional Trends. By 2015, many Latin American countries will enjoy greater prosperity as a result of expanding hemispheric and global economic links, the information revolution, and lowered birthrates. Progress in building democratic institutions will reinforce reform and promote prosperity by enhancing investor confidence. Brazil and Mexico will be increasingly confident and capable actors that will seek a greater voice in hemispheric affairs. But the region will remain vulnerable to financial crises because of its dependence on external finance and the continuing role of single commodities in most economies. The weakest countries in the region, especially in the Andean region, will fall further behind. Reversals of democracy in some countries will be spurred by a failure to deal effectively with popular demands, crime, corruption, drug trafficking, and insurgencies.

Latin America—especially Venezuela, Mexico, and Brazil—will become an increasingly important oil producer by 2015 and an important component of the emerging Atlantic Basin energy system. Its proven oil reserves are second only to those located in the Middle East.

Globalization Gains and Limits. Continued trade and investment liberalization and the expansion of free trade agreements within and outside of Latin America will be a significant catalyst of growth. Regional trade integration through organizations such as MERCOSUR and the likely conclusion of a Free Trade Area of the Americas will both boost employment and provide the political context for governments to sustain economic reforms even against opposing entrenched interest groups.

Latin America's Internet market is poised to grow exponentially, stimulating commerce, foreign investment, new jobs, and corporate efficiency. Although Internet business opportunities will promote the growth of firms throughout the region, Brazil, Argentina, and Mexico are likely to be the biggest beneficiaries.

Shifting Demographics. Latin America's demographics will shift markedly—to the distinct advantage of some countries—helping to ease social strains and underpin higher economic growth. During the next 15 years, most countries will experience a substantial slowdown in the number of new jobseekers, which will help reduce unemployment and boost wages. But not all countries will enjoy these shifts; Bolivia, Ecuador, Guatemala, Honduras, Nicaragua, and Paraguay will still face rapidly increasing populations in need of work.

Democratization Progress and Setbacks. By 2015, key countries will have made some headway in building sturdier and more capable democratic institutions. Democratic institutions in Mexico, Argentina, Chile, and Brazil appear poised for continued incremental consolidation. In other countries, crime, public corruption, the spread of poverty, and the failure of governments to redress worsening income inequality will provide fertile ground for populist and authoritarian politicians. Soaring crime rates will contribute to vigilantism and extrajudicial killings by the police. Burgeoning criminal

activity—including money laundering, alien smuggling, and narcotrafficking—could overwhelm some Caribbean countries. Democratization in Cuba will depend upon how and when Fidel Castro passes from the scene.

Growing Regional Gaps. By 2015, the gap between the more prosperous and democratic states of Latin America and the others will widen. Countries that are unable or unwilling to undertake reforms will experience slow growth at best. Several will struggle intermittently with serious domestic political and economic problems such as crime, corruption, and dependence on single commodities such as oil. Countries with high crime and widespread corruption will lack the political consensus to advance economic reforms and will face lower growth prospects. Although poverty and inequality will remain endemic throughout the region, high-fertility countries will face higher rates of poverty and unemployment.

The Andean countries—Colombia, Venezuela, Ecuador, and Peru—are headed for greater challenges of differing nature and origin. Competition for scarce resources, demographic pressures, and a lack of employment opportunities probably will cause workers' anger to mount and fuel more aggressive tactics in the future. Fatigue with economic hardship and deep popular cynicism about political institutions, particularly traditional parties, could lead to instability in Venezuela, Peru and Ecuador. Resolution of the long-running guerrilla war is key to Colombia's future prospects. The Cuban economy under a Castro Government will fall further behind most of the Latin American countries that embrace globalization and adopt free market practices.

Rising Migration. Pressures for legal and illegal migration to the United States and regionally will rise during the next 15 years. Demographic factors, political instability, personal insecurity, poverty, wage differentials, the growth of alien-smuggling networks, and wider family ties will propel more Latin American workers to enter the United States. El Salvador, Guatemala, Honduras, and Nicaragua will become even greater sources of illegal migrants. In Mexico, declining population growth and strong economic prospects will gradually diminish pressures to seek work in the United States, but disparities in living standards, US demand for labor, and family ties will remain strong pull factors. Significant political instability during a transition process in Cuba could lead to mass migration.

• The growth of Central American and Mexican alien-smuggling networks will exacerbate problems along the US border.

Illegal migration within the region will become a more contentious issue between Latin American governments. Argentina and Venezuela already have millions of undocumented workers from neighboring countries, and resentment of illegal workers could increase. Although most Haitian migrants will head for the United States, Haiti's Caribbean neighbors will also experience further strains.

Significant Discontinuities

The trends outlined in this study are based on the combinations of drivers that are most likely over the next 15 years. Nevertheless, the drivers could produce trends quite different from the ones described. Below are possibilities different from those presented in the body of the study:

• Serious deterioration of living standards for the bulk of the population in several major Middle Eastern countries and the failure of Israel and the Palestinians to conclude even a "cold peace," lead to serious, violent political upheavals in Egypt, Jordan, and Saudi Arabia.

• The trend toward more diverse, free-wheeling transnational terrorist networks leads to the formation of an international terrorist coalition with diverse anti-Western objectives and access to WMD.

• Another global epidemic on the scale of HIV/AIDS, or rapidly changing weather patterns attributable to global warming, with grave damage and enormous costs for several developed countries—sparking an enduring global consensus on the need for concerted action on health issues and the environment.

• A state of major concern to US strategic interests—such as Iran, Nigeria, Israel, or Saudi Arabia—fails to manage serious internal religious or ethnic divisions and crisis ensues.

• A growing antiglobalization movement becomes a powerful sustainable global political and cultural force—threatening Western governmental and corporate interests.

• China, India, and Russia form a defacto geo-strategic alliance in an attempt to counterbalance US and Western influence.

• The US-European alliance collapses, owing in part to intensifying trade disputes and competition for leadership in handling security questions.

• Major Asian countries establish an Asian Monetary Fund or less likely an Asian Trade Organization, undermining the IMF and WTO and the ability of the US to exercise global economic leadership.

(U) Appendix

Four Alternative Global Futures

In September-October 1999, the NIC initiated work on *Global Trends 2015* by cosponsoring with Department of State/INR and CIA's Global Futures Project two unclassified workshops on *Alternative Global Futures: 2000-2015*. The workshops brought together several dozen government and nongovernment specialists in a wide range of fields.

The first workshop identified major factors and events that would drive global change through 2015. It focused on demography, natural resources, science and technology, the global economy, governance, social/cultural identities, and conflict and identified main trends and regional variations. These analyses became the basis for subsequent elaboration in *Global Trends 2015*.

The second workshop developed four alternative global futures in which these drivers would interact in different ways through 2015. Each scenario was intended to construct a plausible, policy-relevant story of how this future might evolve: highlighting key uncertainties, discontinuities, and unlikely or "wild card" events, and identifying important policy and intelligence challenges.

Scenario One: Inclusive Globalization:
A virtuous circle develops among technology, economic growth, demographic factors, and effective governance, which enables a majority of the world's people to benefit from globalization. **Technological** development and diffusion—in some cases triggered by severe environmental or health crises—are utilized to

grapple effectively with some problems of the developing world. Robust global **economic growth**—spurred by a strong policy consensus on economic liberalization—diffuses wealth widely and mitigates many demographic and resource problems. **Governance** is effective at both the national and international levels. In many countries, the state's role shrinks, as its functions are privatized or performed by public-private partnerships, while global cooperation intensifies on many issues through a variety of international arrangements. **Conflict** is minimal within and among states benefiting from globalization. A minority of the world's people—in Sub-Saharan Africa, the Middle East, Central and South Asia, and the Andean region—do not benefit from these positive changes, and internal conflicts persist in and around those countries left behind.

Scenario Two: Pernicious Globalization
Global elites thrive, but the majority of the world's population fails to benefit from globalization. **Population growth and resource scarcities** place heavy burdens on many developing countries, and migration becomes a major source of interstate tension. **Technologies** not only fail to address the problems of developing countries but also are exploited by negative and illicit networks and incorporated into destabilizing weapons. The global **economy** splits into three: growth continues in developed countries; many developing countries experience low or negative per capita growth, resulting in a growing gap with the

developed world; and the illicit economy grows dramatically. **Governance** and political leadership are weak at both the national and international levels. Internal **conflicts** increase, fueled by frustrated expectations, inequities, and heightened communal tensions; WMD proliferate and are used in at least one internal conflict.

Scenario Three: Regional Competition
Regional identities sharpen in Europe, Asia, and the Americas, driven by growing political resistance in Europe and East Asia to US global preponderance and US-driven globalization and each region's increasing preoccupation with its own economic and political priorities. There is an uneven diffusion of **technologies**, reflecting differing regional concepts of intellectual property and attitudes towards biotechnology. Regional **economic** integration in trade and finance increases, resulting in both fairly high levels of economic growth and rising regional competition. Both the state and institutions of regional **governance** thrive in major developed and emerging market countries, as governments recognize the need to resolve pressing regional problems and shift responsibilities from global to regional institutions. Given the preoccupation of the three major regions with their own concerns, countries outside these regions in Sub-Saharan Africa, the Middle East, and Central and South Asia have few places to turn for resources or political support. Military **conflict** among and within the three major regions does not materialize, but internal conflicts increase in and around other countries left behind.

Scenario Four: Post-Polar World
US domestic preoccupation increases as the US **economy** slows, then stagnates. Economic and political tensions with Europe grow, the US-European alliance deteriorates as the United States withdraws its troops, and Europe turns inward, relying on its own regional institutions. At the same time, national **governance** crises create instability in Latin America, particularly in Colombia, Cuba, Mexico, and Panama, forcing the United States to concentrate on the region. Indonesia also faces internal crisis and risks disintegration, prompting China to provide the bulk of an ad hoc peacekeeping force. Otherwise, Asia is generally prosperous and stable, permitting the United States to focus elsewhere. Korea's normalization and *de facto* unification proceed, China and Japan provide the bulk of external financial support for Korean unification, and the United States begins withdrawing its troops from Korea and Japan. Over time, these geostrategic shifts ignite longstanding national rivalries among the Asian powers, triggering increased military preparations and hitherto dormant or covert WMD programs. Regional and global institutions prove irrelevant to the evolving **conflict** situation in Asia, as China issues an ultimatum to Japan to dismantle its nuclear program and Japan—invoking its bilateral treaty with the US—calls for US reengagement in Asia under adverse circumstances at the brink of a major war. Given the priorities of Asia, the Americas, and Europe, countries outside these regions are marginalized, with virtually no sources of political or financial support.

Generalizations Across the Scenarios
The four scenarios can be grouped in two pairs: the first pair contrasting the "positive" and "negative" effects of globalization; the second pair contrasting intensely competitive but not conflictual regionalism and the descent into regional military conflict.

- In all but the first scenario, globalization does not create widespread global cooperation. Rather, in the second scenario, globalization's negative effects promote extensive dislocation and conflict, while in the third and fourth, they spur regionalism.

- In all four scenarios, countries negatively affected by population growth, resource scarcities and bad governance, fail to benefit from globalization, are prone to internal conflicts, and risk state failure.

- In all four scenarios, the effectiveness of national, regional, and international governance and at least moderate but steady economic growth are crucial.

- In all four scenarios, US global influence wanes.

Driver Behavior in the Global Futures Scenarios

	Scenario: Inclusive Globalization	Scenario: Pernicious Globalization	Scenario: Regional Competition	Scenario: Post-Polar World
Population	Global population increases by 1 billion people. Pressures from population growth mitigated by high average annual economic growth. Urbanization manageable in many countries, but some cities with rapid population growth become politically unstable. High migration beneficial for sending and receiving countries, although controversial in Europe and Japan.	Additional 1 billion people prove burdensome for many developing countries, due to slow economic growth and regional protectionism. Inadequate urban infrastructure and social services in most cities create conditions ripe for instability and insurgency. South–North migration becomes major source of tension, spurring US and Europe to disengage from developing countries.	Additional 1 billion people become unstable for many developing countries, due to slow economic growth and regional protectionism. Cities in many developing countries become unstable, due to growing economic disparities, inadequate infrastructure and services, and weak governance; increasing cross-border migration.	Additional 1 billion people destabilizing some countries, such as Indonesia, and make arctic rapidly growing ethics ungovernable. Population dynamics create opportunities for China and emerging market countries of Latin America and contribute to tendering of great-power relationships in Asia.
Resources	Population increases and robust economic growth will stress all systems, resulting in soil degradation, CO_2 pollution, deforestation and loss of species, especially in areas of rapid urbanization. Advanced developing economies largely resolve resource problems although the poorest developing countries will suffer resource scarcities. In particular, water scarcities will worsen in South Asia, northern China, Middle East, and Africa.	Population growth will contribute to scarcities of arable land and fresh water, exacerbated by inappropriate policies of subsidy and protectionism. Resource scarcities particularly that of fresh water, will be major problems on both emerging market and developing countries, reducing agricultural production and spurring migration to cities.	Population growth, economic pressures, and policy failures create resource scarcities, especially in poor countries and highly populated emerging markets. International environmental collaboration weakens, and local conflicts over water spur cross-border migration.	Resource trends similar to those on regional competition scenario.
Technology	Conditions will be auspicious for rapid innovation, diffusion and implementation of IT breakthroughs, and smart materials. IT will resource productivity gains and higher levels of non-inflationary growth for many countries. Some countries will fall further behind because they lack sufficient education levels, infrastructure, and regulatory systems.	Innovation and diffusion will be slow, due to economic stagnation and political uncertainties. The destabilizing effects of technology will predominate: WMD proliferates; IT empowers terrorists and criminals. Benefits of technology will be realized by only a few rich countries, while most countries will fall further behind.	Technology advances and commercializes rapidly, but regional protectionism reduces economies of scale and promotes trade barriers. Conflicts over market openings for high technology sectors break out. Developing countries unable to compete in global economy fall into technological backwardness.	Widespread regional protectionism and conflicts over access to high technology develop. Regional and great-power relations in Asia become more contentious. Demand for militarily-relevant technologies in Asia increases.
Economy	US global leadership and economic power further liberalization of trade, broad acceptance of market reform, rapid diffusion of IT, and absence of great-power conflict will generate on average 4% annual global economic growth. Emerging markets—China, India, Brazil—and many developing countries will benefit. Some states in Africa, the Middle East, Andean region, Central Asia and the Caucasus will lag.	A US downturn leads to economic stagnation. Global consensus supporting market reforms will erode, undermining the "American economic model," making US especially vulnerable and leading US to disengage from global involvement. Emerging markets, as well as most developing countries, are hard hit by economic stagnation.	Growth is robust, but diminished by effects of regionalism and protectionism. US maintains advantage over Europe and Japan through ability to absorb foreign workers. Emerging markets are targets of developed country mercantilist competition. Other developing countries are neglected by rich countries and atrophied global institutions.	Economic trends similar to those in regional competition scenario.
Identity and Governance	Ethnic background, challenges achievement of some states, engrave workers create chronic tensions in ethnically heterogeneous Europe and East Asia, and communal tensions and violence increase in developing countries with poor governance. In many states benefiting from rapid economic growth and spread of IT, function of governance will diffuse widely from national governments to local governments and partnerships with business firms, non-profits. Some states' capacity to govern will weaken, and especially in the Andean region, Sub-Saharan Africa, and Central and South Asia.	Ethnic/religious identities sharpest in many heterogeneous states. Communal tensions and violence increase in Africa, Central and South Asia, and parts of Middle East. Political Islam grows. Likelihood of terrorism against targets linked to globalization and the US will increase, hastening Northern disengagement. Weakening of governing capacity at all levels among both developed and developing countries; China and Russia face territorial fragmentation.	Globalization, assertiveness of US "hegemony," and cultural changes challenge national identities, contributing to US–European and US–Asian estrangement and increasing US engagement in Latin America. Labor mobility sharpens ethnic/religious identities in countries where immigrants cannot be absorbed. Communal pressures in developing countries increase, in some cases leading to internal communal conflicts. Mercantilist competition strengthens the state. A number of regional organizations are strengthened while global institutions weaken, due to institution, preoccupation with domestic/regional issues, and EU/Japan resentment of US governance.	Globalization and cultural changes contribute to US–European estrangement and increase US engagement in Latin America. Traditional national identities and rivalries stoke intensified nationalism in Asia. Labor mobility sharpens ethnic/religious identities in countries where immigrants cannot be absorbed. Communal pressures increase in many developing countries; and conflicts persist in the Andean region, Indonesia, and elsewhere. Both mercantilist competition and a growing prospect of interstate conflict in Asia strengthen developed and emerging market states' ability to command resources, invest in militarily-relevant technology, and control borders. Both global and regional intergovernmental institutions weaken.
Conflict	Absence of great-power conflict. Conflict is minimal between and within developed and emerging market countries, due to economic prosperity and growing acceptance of democratic norms. Internal and cross-border conflicts persist in Sub-Saharan Africa, parts of Central, South and Southeast Asia, and the Andean region due to lack of effective governance and countries' inability to handle population growth, resources scarcities, ethnic tensions, and urbanization. Developed countries will allow many strategically remote conflicts to proceed without attempting to intervene.	Risk of regional conflict in Asia rises substantially. Serious questions arise concerning: • China's territorial integrity, • India's ability to govern, • Future of democracy in Russia. Frequency of internal and interstate conflicts increases, triggered by rising tensions in emerging and developing countries and reduced cooperation among developed countries. WMD restraints will erode, increasing risks of terrorism and regional aggression.	Increased regionalism results in conflict over markets, investment flows, and resources, further reducing international collaboration on terrorism, crime, cross-border conflicts, and WMD proliferation. WMD proliferates rapidly and dangerously. High levels of internal and cross-border conflicts persist in developing countries.	As US concentrates on Western Hemisphere and downgrades its presence in Europe and Asia, China drives towards regional dominance. Japan reasserts and the risk of great-power conflict increases as US contemplates reasserting influence in Asia. WMD proliferates rapidly and dangerously, particularly in Asia. High levels of internal and cross-border conflicts persist in developing countries.

DI Design Center 376666AA 10-00

The National Intelligence Council

The National Intelligence Council (NIC) manages the Intelligence Community's estimative process, incorporating the best available expertise inside and outside the government. It reports to the Director of Central Intelligence in his capacity as head of the US Intelligence Community and speaks authoritatively on substantive issues for the Community as a whole.

Chairman (concurrently Assistant Director of Central Intelligence for Analysis and Production)	John Gannon	(703) 482-6724
Vice Chairman	Ellen Laipson	(703) 482-3578
Director, Senior Review, Production, and Analysis	Stuart A. Cohen	(703) 482-0741

National Intelligence Officers

Africa	Robert Houdek	(703) 482-7225
At-Large	Stuart A. Cohen	(703) 482-0741
Conventional Military Issues	John Landry	(703) 482-7105
East Asia	Robert Sutter	(703) 482-5721
Economics & Global Issues	David Gordon	(703) 482-4128
Europe	Barry F. Lowenkron	(703) 482-6295
Latin America	Fulton T. Armstrong	(703) 482-3136
Near East and South Asia	Paul Pillar	(703) 482-6833
Russia and Eurasia	George Kolt	(703) 482-6297
Science & Technology	Lawrence Gershwin	(703) 482-6811
Strategic & Nuclear Programs	Robert D Walpole	(703) 482-7424
Warning	Robert Vickers	(703) 482-0993

CPSIA information can be obtained at www.ICGtesting.com
Printed in the USA
BVOW07s2146061115

426043BV00015B/238/P